CLAYSHOOTING

CLAYSHOOTING

A complete guide to Skeet, Trap and Sporting Shooting

Peter Croft

WARD LOCK

First published 1990 by Ward Lock
Artillery House, Artillery Row,
London SW1P 1RT, England

A Cassell imprint

© Peter Croft 1990

Photography by John Best

**British Library Cataloguing in
Publication Data**
Croft, Peter
  Clay shooting.
  1. Clay pigeon shooting – Manuals
  I. Title
  799.3'13

  ISBN 0–7063–6763–4

Printed and bound in Great Britain by
Butler & Tanner Ltd, Frome and London

CONTENTS

THE HISTORY OF CLAYSHOOTING

The earliest shotgun shooting competitions involved the shooting of live pigeons released from boxes (known as traps). Live pigeon shooting developed originally in and around London at gun clubs such as Hornsey and Notting Hill. It soon became an accepted part of the shooting scene. As it grew in popularity, it rapidly spread throughout the British Empire and into Europe and the United States. Prize money grew and many competitions were the subject of huge personal wagers among those taking part.

Initially competitors used percussion muzzle-loading guns, but in the mid 1880s the breech-loader appeared, and it was not long before it was adopted by the competitive live pigeon shooter. Gunmakers built specialist live pigeon guns and were quick to advertise any successes achieved with their products. Special cartridges were loaded and, again, their successes were extensively publicized. Some shooters made a good living out of their prowess at the traps and a few achieved widespread fame.

This interest in competitive shotgun shooting soon led to a search for an inanimate target to replace the unfortunate pigeon. The use of glass balls as a substitute for live birds was introduced by Charles Portlock of Boston in 1836. These glass balls were made of smooth glass about 2½in in diameter. Coloured glass was tried to make the balls more visible and the surfaces of the balls were checkered to make them break more readily. Many other materials were used experimentally; one enterprising gentleman made birds of tin, and the call of 'dead bird' was made by the referee if the shot charge moved the target from its flightpath. The advantage claimed by the inventor was that they could be used again and again, but so many arguments arose that this tin target was soon discarded. Another innovation was to fill glass balls with feathers to make it easier to judge when a target was hit. This was not entirely successful since the glass balls were not always consistent: sometimes they broke on throwing; at other times they were so hard they wouldn't break when struck squarely by the shot charge. More importantly, they could not replicate the speed and flight of the pigeon and they consequently presented the shooter with a far less testing mark for the gun. Prodigious scores were recorded with glass balls in exhibition matches in the United States, by the shooting legends 'Doc' Carver and Captain Adam Bogardus, with few, if any, targets being missed. So, although the glass ball was used extensively for a short period, the search was still on for a target that could approach the pigeon in terms of difficulty.

This resulted in the development of the clay pigeon around 1880. This is generally credited to the American, George Ligowsky of Cincinnati, but at the same time an Englishman named McCaskey came up with a similar design. Regardless of who invented it, the clay pigeon had arrived, and was an immediate success. The flight of the clay was uniform and resembled a bird in flight. The first ones were made entirely of clay and this name stuck even though targets today have no clay in them. The clay was pressed into a mould and baked in a kiln like a brick. (Sometimes this resulted in targets so hard that they would not break even when struck in the densest part of the pattern!) Improvements were made in the raw material and a combination of pitch and limestone was found to be the most satisfactory. Improvements are still being made and some makers are experimenting with the use of waste materials from manufacturing processes as a source of raw materials.

The shooting of live pigeons released from traps came under increased pressure from the protectionist lobby and was gradually outlawed in various states in America around the turn of the century. In Britain it was finally banned by the **Captive Birds (Prohibition of Shooting) Act 1921** after a vigorous campaign led by the *Daily Express*. There is a story that a pigeon, wounded in a competition, fell dead in the Princess Royal's carriage and that it was this that finally prompted the sport's demise. Today, competition live pigeon shooting still takes place in one or two mediterranean countries and in Latin America.

As competition live pigeon shooting was declining, clay pigeons were in the ascendancy. In 1900 the American Trapshooting Association was formed to govern the sport in the United States, and a little earlier the Inanimate Bird Shooting Association had been formed in Britain. Both these associations had a short life. The Inanimate Bird Shooting Association became the Clay Pigeon Shooting Association and with the support of cartridge makers Eley-Kynoch (as they were then known) developed into the CPSA as we know it today. (Eley withdrew its support in the early 1970s but by then the CPSA was able to survive on its own. There is no doubt that Eley's contribution over the years, together with that of Peter Page, the secretary and first Director of the CPSA, ensured the growth and development of clayshooting as a sport.)

The American Trapshooting Association was superseded in 1924 by the Amateur Trapshooting Association, which did much to clean up some of the abuses that were creeping into the sport. Today the ATA is probably the largest clay target governing body in the world. Each year it organizes the Grand American Tournament at its headquarters in Vandalia, Ohio. This is undoubtedly the largest Down-the-Line shoot in the world with a line of trap ranges that stretches for over one mile (1½km).

From these early beginnings, clay-shooting has developed into a world-wide sport of many different disciplines. Two of these Olympic Trap and Olympic Skeet, are part of the Olympic programme, and are also competed for at Continental and World Championship level. Universal Trap and FITASC Sporting also have World and European Championships, so there is no lack of opportunity for the shooter who aspires to represent his country.

The attraction of clayshooting as a sport is that it can be all things to all men (or women). It ranges from fun shooting at small local clubs, through county and national events and the international level of Continental and World Championships, to the pinnacle of the Olympic Games. At all these different levels it is an interesting, challenging and enjoyable sport. Age is no prohibition to participation, and people from all walks of life obtain a great deal of enjoyment from shooting clay targets. It is also possible for the relative novice to compete alongside Olympic and World Champions, unlike the majority of other Olympic sports.

In writing this book, I have endeavoured to explain the various forms of clayshooting and the methods I have found successful in competition. It is not a definitive work; nor do I claim my way is the only way. Some very successful shooters use different techniques from my own, with excellent results. Who am I to say they are wrong? My main aim in writing this book is to attempt to short-circuit some of the frustration felt in becoming a successful competition shooter at whatever level.

After an initial lesson to set me off on the right foot at Joe Carey's Shooting School near Ledbury in Herefordshire (at the tender age of eleven), much of my shooting technique has been self-taught. In learning for myself, I made many technical mistakes and wasted an awful lot of time doing things wrong. If this book saves the reader making just one of these mistakes and saves them a bit of that wasted time (and money!) then it will have been worthwhile. Remember, no one is born with the ability to shoot. It is a skill that requires guidance and practice to develop.

GUNS

In order to shoot you require a gun. An obvious statement, but one that should be qualified by the word 'suitable'. When I look around at the many shoots I attend, I see countless people attempting to compete with totally unsuitable guns. A great many of the beginners who come to our shooting school are similarly ill-equipped. There are a number of reasons for this: lack of funds, poor advice and, sometimes, unscrupulous salesmanship. The gun is your biggest single investment in the sport of clayshooting, and in order to be successful at whatever level you intend to compete, it is vital that you acquire a suitable and reliable weapon.

I started my clayshooting career with my grandfather's gun, an anonymous Birmingham box-lock side-by-side at the age of fourteen. It was the only gun I had, so it had to do: I even managed to win a couple of trophies with it. Winning these small shoots gave me the taste for bigger competitions, so I entered the Cardiganshire Down-the-Line (DTL) Championship. This was a little like entering the RAC Rally in a Reliant Robin. The barrels got extremely hot and burnt my left hand, for the first time I suffered bruising on my face and shoulder, and the final score was a disaster! It didn't require much intelligence to work out that I needed something more appropriate if I was going to make my mark in the world of clayshooting.

That day at Felinfach, I spent a lot of time examining the other competitors' guns and it was obvious that the most popular and successful shotgun was the under-and-over. There followed a period of intense family negotiation which culminated in my being allowed to exchange a 20-bore side-by-side for an under-and-over. Problem solved? Sadly, no. Because I lacked any real knowledge of clayshooting, I marched off to the local gunmaker to examine his selection of under-and-overs. I had decided that I was going to shoot DTL, and therefore needed a gun with a healthy degree of choke. I settled on a Franchi with 28in barrels bored full and ½ choke with double triggers! From a Reliant Robin to a Ford Anglia. I didn't realize the advantages of the single trigger and knew nothing of the differences between a game gun stock and a Trap gun stock. Once again I had an unsuitable gun, as I soon discovered when I entered a 50 bird DTL match at Bridgenorth Gun Club in Shropshire. Proudly wielding my new under-and-over, I shot a score worse than any I had shot with Grandad's old side-by-side.

Where had I gone wrong? My most basic mistake had been to go to a firm of gunmakers who knew nothing about clayshooting. What they had sold me was a game gun, one that I could use very effectively for game shooting, but a Trap gun it was not. This was no reflection on the firm that had sold it to me: they didn't understand the differences in competition guns and I was so keen to get an under-and-over that I grabbed the first one offered. My own lack of knowledge, and that of the gunmakers, had left me just as ill-equipped as when I started. Back to the drawing board.

I now sat down and had a complete rethink. It was obvious that I had insufficient knowledge of the sport to make an informed choice. It was equally obvious that not all gun dealers understood the technicalities of clayshooting. I looked around for a dealer whose name appeared regularly in the competition results in the magazine *Shooting Times*, and I settled on Ian Coley, who in those days managed Fletcher's gun shop in Gloucester. Ian had a formidable shooting reputation on the Midlands clay circuit. I travelled down to Gloucester, and after much good advice from Ian traded the Franchi in for a Miroku Trap gun. Nearly six

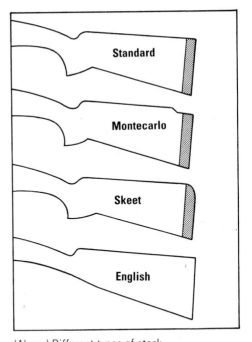

(Above) Different types of stock

(Below) Sideplates allow scope for engravers to transform guns into works of art.

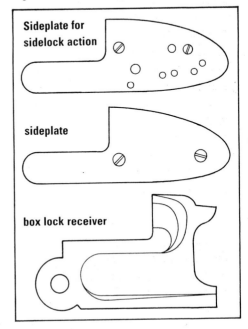

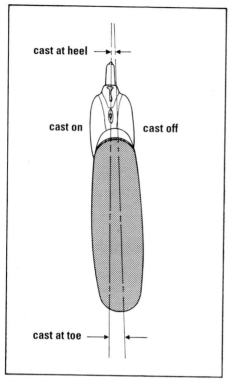

The gunfitter calculates the 'cast' at heel and toe, as indicated.

sport has also led to an increase in the number of gun dealers, some of whom lack the knowledge and experience to advise the budding clayshooter on his choice of gun.

When you are ready to purchase your first gun, or upgrade your present one, find a dealer who is an experienced competitor in your discipline. Tell him how much you can afford to spend and listen to his advice. It is always helpful to patronize a dealer who has access to shooting facilities where you can try guns before you part with the money. Virtually all clayshooting specialists offer this service. It is in their interest to sell you the most suitable gun for your chosen discipline and your personal style of shooting. A happy customer will always come back and will also recommend the dealer to his friends.

years after I had shot my first DTL target, I became the proud owner of a suitable Trap gun. Trapshooting suddenly became much easier and my scores showed a huge increase.

The purpose in relating this story is to try to prevent you from making similar mistakes and wasting time at the beginning of your shooting career. Today, the chances of acquiring an unsuitable gun are much greater. As the sport has grown in popularity there has been a proliferation of cheap and, in some cases nasty, guns that are totally inappropriate for clay target shooting. The growth in the

TYPES OF COMPETITION GUN

Shotguns are built with a variety of different actions and mechanisms: under-and-over, side-by-side, box-lock and side-lock, semi-automatic, pump-action, bolt-action and single barrel. However, the under-and-over and the semi-automatic are the only two options for serious competition work. The one exception to this is American Trapshooting (ATA), where only one shot is allowed at single rise targets, and pump-action or high quality single barrel Trap guns may be used as there is no requirement for a second shot.

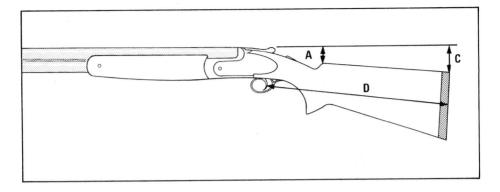

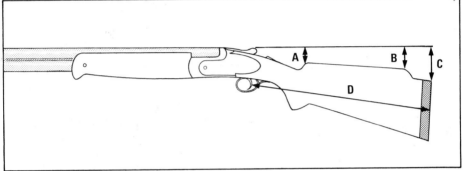

The vital statistics: **A** drop at comb; **B** drop at rear of comb; **C** drop at heel; **D** length.

For all other disciplines where two shots are fired, the two options of under-and-over or semi-automatic apply. Of the two, there is no doubt that the best choice is the under-and-over. Since its development by the top London gunmakers at the turn of the century, it has been constantly refined and developed into the competition gun of today. When John M. Browning designed the B25 in the 1920s, he brought the under-and-over within the financial reach of a much greater number of people than ever before. Such companies as Miroku and Beretta furthered this by applying mass-production techniques to the design. The result is an extensive range of affordable under-and-overs for today's shooter.

There are a vast number of under-and-overs on the market, some of which are of dubious quality and design. The best advice is to select a gun from a manufacturer with an established reputation in competition shooting. If the model you desire is outside your price range, look around for a good second-hand one. A used gun made by one of the major manufacturers is a much better proposition than a cheap weapon from some obscure maker whose quality is dictated by price. Many of the cheap under-and-overs have stocks of unusable dimensions. In addition, because they are built down to a price, the quality of the materials used is often poor. Remember, a competition gun gets a lot of heavy use even if you only shoot at your local club. A gun that can stand up to the limited use of rough shooting will often collapse under the heavy use of clayshooting. Therefore go for quality — if necessary second-hand quality — in preference to new rubbish.

The under-and-over

This is without doubt the most popular form of competition shotgun worldwide. The majority of under-and-overs utilize a variation of the Blitz or trigger plate action. They are not box-locks, although incorrectly described as such. In fact, they have much in common with the renowned Dickson Round Action. One of the advantages of using trigger plate actions is that they can be made detachable. The ability to change the trigger mechanism instantly can be a great advantage when a mainspring breaks at a critical stage in a competition. Currently Perazzi and Gamba offer this option, whilst Beretta has prototypes under development and should be offering a detachable action gun in the near future. Naturally guns with this facility tend to be more expensive, but they are well worth the money when competing at top level. It's hard to put a price on peace of mind.

Most under-and-overs are equipped with a single trigger. This enables a rapid second shot to be fired without relocating the trigger finger or the

Measuring a competition gun for cast, drop and pitch.

hand. This is obviously of great benefit where a fast and accurate second shot is required. Most single triggers are of the selective variety, usually utilizing the safety catch as a barrel selector. A selective trigger

14

can be of great benefit on the Sporting clay gun, particularly when used for the de-anding FITASC form of the sport. However, if your discipline is Trap or Skeet, a selective single trigger is superfluous since it is unnecessary to change the firing sequence on a Trap or Skeet gun. Indeed, some of the top manufacturers, such as Perazzi and Beretta, routinely fit non-selective single triggers on their quality Trap and Skeet guns.

The leading manufacturers between them offer an extensive range of under-and-overs designed for each specific discipline. It is largely a matter of selecting one in your price range that suits you and suits the discipline concerned.

The semi-automatic

The semi-auto shotgun, or automatic, as it is more commonly known is quite popular with a number of shooters. There are two principal reasons for this. One is cost: automatics are built entirely by machine so it is possible to make a quality automatic shotgun for a price comparable to the cheapest under-and-overs. In this respect the auto offers conspicuous value for money. The second popular feature is the lack of apparent recoil, particularly in the gas-operated versions. This makes the automatic a good choice for beginners and for women. It considerably reduces the amount of physical punishment caused by poor gun mounting, and is more comfortable for shooters of slight build.

Semi-automatics do have their disadvantages, however, the main one being their reliability. Due to their complexity, they must be carefully maintained or malfunctions will occur. Another slight disadvantage is the lack of choice of choke, as there is only one barrel. For Skeet this is unimportant, but it could be a problem in Sporting, although the international successes of Duncan Lawton with his Remington 1100 would seem to disprove this.

The problem of reliability can be overcome by always carrying an identical spare gun, a tactic which can be equally applied to the under-and-over. When competing at international level, the serious competitor will travel with a pair of matching guns. It is amazing what airlines can do to the most carefully packed guns and mechanical faults usually develop in the most obscure locations. If you are shooting in the Mongolian Championship it's reassuring to know that if your favourite gun breaks down you have an identical one to fall back on. It's significant that the shooters from three of the world's top Trapshooting nations — Italy, USA and East Germany — always take two guns each when competing internationally.

Ribs

Whichever design of gun you opt for it will almost certainly have a ventilated rib. The ventilations are vital in helping to reduce the heat haze above the barrels which occurs when a large number of shots are

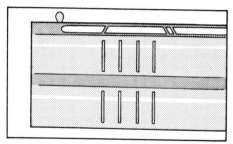

Perazzi Skeet guns have muzzel brakes, four slots cut into the barrel to reduce recoil and 'muzzle flip'.

fired in rapid succession. This is a particular problem when shooting in a hot climate but don't forget we do occasionally get scorching hot days in Britain. Some guns have a stepped ventilated rib but I personally fail to see any merit in such an arrangement. I feel that the step in the rib can be a visual distraction, causing the shooter to look at the rib instead of concentrating his vision on the target. There are many different widths of rib provided by the various manufacturers which all have their followers and are equally efficient. It is really a matter of personal choice. My own preference is for a rib of 10 or 11mm with a central sighting line of 3mm. The line down the centre is not necessary — it's just that most of my guns have it and I like it!

Gauge

Before 1989 there would have been no question as to the calibre of a competition shotgun. It would have been 12-gauge and nothing but 12-gauge. As from 1989 the rules for

disciplines under the jurisdiction of the International Shooting Union (ISU) limit the permitted shot load to 28g (approximately 1oz), reducing it from 32g. Most of the other disciplines followed in 1990. This opens up interesting possibilities for the 20-gauge gun in serious competition. Some of the Italian cartridge manufacturers have already developed 28g 20-gauge loads that can match the performance of the 28g load in 12-gauge.

When I was first told of this my initial reaction was one of disbelief. Having been raised on the teachings of such notable ballisticians as Burrard and Gough Thomas I didn't believe that a 20-gauge could match a 12-gauge. To convince me, Mauro Perazzi took me on to the pattern range at the Perazzi factory and we patterned my MX8 Trap gun against an experimental 20-gauge Perazzi Trap gun, using 28g Baschieri & Pellagri F2 loads in both 12- and 20-gauge. The results surprised me. There was nothing to choose between the 12- and the 20- as regards pattern percentage or pattern quality. Mauro then invited me to try the 20- on the factory's private Olympic Trap range. Although the gun was rather lighter than I am used to, I found no problem in shooting good scores with it.

The benefits of this development could be enormous for youngsters and women. It would enable a shooter of slight build to use a lighter gun, with comparable performance to a 12- and without undue recoil.

16

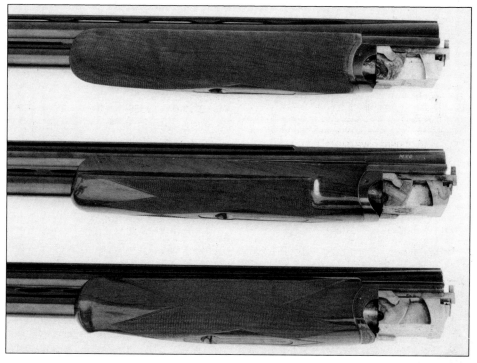

Different styles of forend.

Perazzi are developing a special 20-gauge version of the MX8 on a reduced frame, and Beretta already offer a 20-gauge version of the 682 Trap gun. For women and juniors, these are well worth considering.

The clayshooting gunmakers

In the early part of this century the only under-and-overs available to the clayshooter were highly priced, hand-built guns from a few top London gunmakers. This all changed due to the genius of one man: John Moses Browning, undoubtedly the most prolific and successful inventor in the history of firearms. In 1925, shortly before his death, he patented the design for an under-and-over shotgun that lent itself to modern production techniques. This was the Model 25, which can rightly be said to be the forerunner of today's competition under-and-over. John M.'s untimely death left the development work on the design to his son, Val Browning. During the ensuing years Val Browning refined the original design and developed a reliable single trigger. With the advice of shooters, a range of competition guns evolved and for many years Browning were the dominant force in clayshooting guns.

17

Gradually other manufacturers took up the challenge and developed their own under-and-overs and more reasonably priced under-and-overs became available.

The boom in clayshooting in the last two decades has led to a proliferation of under-and-overs on the clayshooting scene. Unfortunately, many of these leave a lot to be desired as serious competition guns. An analysis of the guns used in major competitions would show that there is a 'Big Five' of competition gun manufacturers: Browning, Perazzi, Beretta, Miroku and Winchester. There is then a second tier of gun manufacturers which include Gamba (and its derivatives such as the Rottweil), Merkel and Vostock. These guns are not as popular as the 'Big Five' but are well designed and have proved successful in international competition.

Browning

The Browning was the first of the affordable under-and-overs. The company offer a range of guns suitable for all forms of clay target shooting. In addition to the Belgian-built Model 25, and its derivative the 125, the company now offers a range of guns manufactured in Japan. These are built to Browning specification, under Browning supervision, and are superb guns for those whose finances don't stretch to the Belgian models. Over the years, Browning products have been used to win an impressive list of major championships at Olympic, World and Continental level. One of Browning's notable successes was when Lancashire vet Bob Braithwaite won the gold medal for Olympic Trap at the 1968 Olympics in Mexico City. Bob used his C3 grade Browning to win the event with a record-equalling score of 198 ex 200. There have been many other notable British victories at international level with the guns, particularly at Sporting, and Brownings are held in high regard by British clayshooters.

Perazzi

Perazzi are relative newcomers on the gunmaking scene as the company was formed in the early 1960s. It brought together the gunmaking skill of Daniele Perazzi and the shooting

F.N. Browning Trapgun.

genius of Ennio Matarelli. Matarelli, who was one of Italy's foremost shooters, collaborated on the design of the Perazzi gun. In 1964, the first year of manufacture, he proved he knew what he was talking about by using the new gun to win the Italian, European, and Olympic Championships in Trap.

The Perazzi action is much shallower than the Browning action, making for a more streamlined gun. This is achieved by the use of bifurcated lumps: a gun built to the Browning design has the lumps situated under the barrels; in the Perazzi, the lumps are machined at either side of the chambers, thus reducing the height of the frame required to accommodate them. This results in a much shallower and stronger action.

Perazzi were the first manufacturer to offer a detachable trigger action and this is a very worthwhile feature of these guns. Murphy's law says that if your gun is going to break a spring, it will choose the most critical time to do it. The ability to effect a

Muzzle brakes.

Barrel porting reduces recoil and muzzle flip.

rapid repair, without dismantling the gun, cannot be overvalued. Anyone owning a shotgun with a detachable trigger assembly should **ALWAYS** carry a spare set of triggers.

Another Perazzi first was in the development of screw-in chokes for under-and-over shotguns. Prior to the Perazzi MT6, the only guns available with interchangeable chokes were automatics and pumps. Daniele Perazzi solved the problem of fitting these chokes to the under-and-over

design in 1975, and now all the major gunmakers offer this option. It is probably fair to say that Perazzi have been the most innovative company in gun design in recent years. As a company they never sit still, always striving to develop the ultimate competition shotgun. One of their strengths is that they have always specialized in competition guns and didn't have to develop existing hunting models for competitive use. The whole set-up is geared to helping the

match shooter and the factory offers a back-up service to the shooter which is second to none.

Currently Perazzi offer a number of models headed by the justly famous MX8. However, there is no standard specification for Perazzi guns. Because the gun is partially hand-built, there is great scope for having a gun made to your own measurements. It is possible to go to the factory in Brescia and have a gun made specially for you at no extra cost. Naturally, Perazzi guns are not cheap but they do offer bespoke gunmaking at a reasonable price.

Perazzi guns are most renowned in the Trap disciplines, but the company also make an excellent range of Skeet and Sporting guns. In the short time they have been making guns, Perazzi have built up an enviable record of success and have won an impressive tally of medals in the hands of shooters from all over the world. It is interesting that, in 1988, all the Great Britain selection shoots, and the British and English Grand Prix in Olympic Trap were won by shooters using Perazzi shotguns. The Perazzi is undoubtedly the ultimate Olympic Trap gun.

Beretta

It is Beretta'a proud boast that they are the world's oldest surviving gunmakers. They date back to the 1600s and today are one of Europe's biggest arms manufacturers. For many years Beretta concentrated its competition gun efforts on the SO side-lock range. Its box-lock (actually trigger plate) guns were basically hunting models and were far from ideal for competitive work. In recent years this has changed completely and much of the credit for this must go to their British agents, Gunmark Ltd. The box-lock range of guns has been revamped considerably and now offers well designed guns for every discipline of clayshooting at a reasonable price. Under development is a gun with a detachable trigger mechanism, the ASE-90, and hopefully this should be available on the British market soon.

In common with Perazzi, its great rival in the lucrative Italian market, Beretta works closely with top

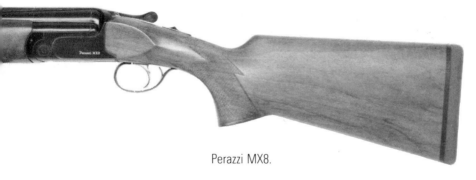

Perazzi MX8.

shooters in the development of its new guns. Two of Britain's top Sporting shooters, Barry Simpson and Brian Hebditch who are both employed by Gunmark, have been very influential in the design of Beretta's excellent range of Sporting clay guns. Both are former International Champions and have a wealth of experience which they have put to good use in developing Beretta's range of shotguns.

Beretta have the distinction of winning more Olympic gold medals in Trapshooting than any other gunmaker (in 1956, 1972, 1980 and 1984). These were all won with the side-lock SO guns but in recent years the 680 series guns have made their mark in international competition.

Miroku

Miroku shotguns have been around for a long time, originally imported into Britain by Millard Bros. The agency subsequently passed to Parker-Hale who did a splendid job of popularizing the marque. In the early 1980s Miroku became closely associated with Browning and the guns are now handled by Browning Sports.

The Miroku is basically a very good Japanese copy of the Browning. Miroku guns have the good handling of the Browning, are built to a high standard, and offer conspicuous value for money. Like the Browning, they are available in a wide variety of styles and finishes to suit all the clayshooting disciplines. One notable feature of the Miroku is the excellent finish of the barrels. The boring and striking up are of the very highest quality. As regards shooting, many of my own international successes were shot with an absolutely standard Miroku 3800 Trap gun. Although relatively cheap compared to some of its competitors, I found nothing lacking in its handling or shooting qualities.

Winchester

Winchester shotguns are, like the Miroku guns, based on the venerable Browning action and are also made in Japan. They have been constantly developed over a number of years and are now one of the best handling Sporting guns on the market. The credit for this development lies with

Miroku Trapgun.

Vic Harker and A. J. 'Smoker' Smith who have worked very hard to produce an improved range of shotguns. Winchester have recently sold off their shotgun making plant in Japan and no longer sell under-and-overs under the Winchester trademark. However all is not lost, since a new company known as Classic Doubles has been formed to continue the Winchesters and the present Classic Doubles gun is a further development of the original Winchester design; in many ways it is a great improvement on an already good design.

The above manufacturers are the 'Big Five', all of which come highly recommended. If you can't afford the model of your choice, look around for a good second-hand one. Better to buy a 'serious' gun to start with than have to chop and change later on.

De-luxe grade guns

Many of the top gunmakers offer their guns in a variety of grades and finishes. Whilst the de-luxe guns look nice, they don't shoot any straighter than the standard models. By all means buy a better grade gun, but you should realize that Galleazzi engraving and exhibition woodwork won't improve your scores. Pride of ownership is a wonderful thing, but at the end of the day a competition gun is a tool, not a work of art.

GUN MAINTENANCE

With modern cartridges gun cleaning is no longer the onerous task it once was. My own recipe for gun cleaning is as follows:

● Before leaving the shoot wipe the gun down and make sure it is dry. Nothing rusts faster than a wet gun in a gun-case.

● On reaching home spray the inside of the barrels with a gun detergent (Beretta, Hoppes or Philips). Stand the barrels in a corner for a few hours and then brush out with a 10-gauge phosphor bronze brush. Lightly oil and put away in a **SECURE** place. Note that the brush is 10-gauge and must be bronze, **NOT** steel. The large

23

diameter of the 10-gauge is more effective in removing plastic residue left by the wadding in modern cartridges.

NEVER slam a gun shut. Always close it gently but firmly. There is no need to slam a gun if it is properly maintained. The gun does not close any more securely and all that you are doing is wearing it out faster.

CARTRIDGES

When I first started clayshooting there was only one specialist Trap cartridge readily available on the British market. That was the Eley Special Trapshooting Cartridge, a paper-cased Kleena wadded shell containing slightly harder shot than the standard game loads sold by Eley. It was loaded in shot sizes 6, 7, 8 and 9, and produced observed velocities of around 1030 fps (feet per second). Virtually all competitors used this cartridge, whatever their discipline and at many championships it was the only shell that was permitted. Contrast this with the vast array of different loads made by a multitude of different manufacturers on offer to today's shooters.

Since those early days there have been many advances in shotgun cartridge design. The first of these was the introduction of the plastic case. Originally developed in the United States, it took a little time to reach Britain. I can well remember the early Remington advertisements for new plastic cartridges. To prove the waterproof qualities of their product, they filled the pockets of a shooting jacket with shells and threw it in a washing machine. The jacket and its load of cartridges were subjected to a multitude of washing cycles. The cartridges were then removed and all chambered and fired successfully. Shooters used to the swelling properties of paper cases were amazed. Today we take plastic cases for granted, and the paper-cased competition cartridge is a comparative rarity.

The next giant step forward was the introduction of the plastic wad. Originally, shotgun cartridges had been loaded with felt wads. In the days of black powder, using best white wool felt wads as an obturator, it had been possible to produce patterns of a very high quality. Unfortunately, the high price of felt wads forced the cartridge manufacturers to look around for a cheaper sustitute, which they found in a kind of fibre board. Whilst this proved an acceptable replacement for the felt wad, it never seemed to produce quite the same quality patterns as the material it superseded. This remained the case until the advent of the plastic wad. Again a transatlantic development, the plastic wad first appeared on this side of the water in Eley's Super Trench cartridge, a 1¼oz load developed for Olympic Trap (before 1974 the maximum shot load at Olympic Trap was 36g or 1¼oz).

This was an immediate success with the Olympic Trench shooters and was a superb cartridge. Other loads followed and today all our domestic loaders put plastic wads in the vast majority of their competition loads.

As I said earlier, when I started clayshooting 90 per cent plus of British clayshooters used Eley. At that time there were few imported cartridges available in the UK and the other loading companies tended to concentrate on game loads. A tragic event in 1973 was to change all this. In November of that year there was an explosion in the Eley loading plant at Witton. Suddenly cartridges were in short supply. This began the influx of continental cartridges that proliferate today. Another factor that increased the sale of imported shells was Winchester's decision to set up a European loading subsidiary in Italy. This enabled the American company to compete on price with the European manufacturers.

Two other major developments in cartridge production have been the introduction of much harder shot, and the continuing improvement in nitro powders. Hard shot, formed by adding antimony to the lead, helps increase the density and quality of the patterns. The harder the shot, the less it is deformed by its passage through the choke portion of the barrel. You can imagine the forces exerted on lead pellets as they are jammed into the constriction at the muzzle of your gun. Soft pellets become deformed; deformed pellets don't fly straight

and become lost to the effective part of the pattern at medium to long range. The modern Trap cartridge is therefore loaded with the harder lead alloy. To further resist deformation, and to prevent cold welding of pellets, some of the better shells are loaded with hard pellets that are coated with a nickel or copper plating. This is not a new idea but can prove very effective in maintaining the even distribution of pellets in the pattern. This is an advantage in the Trap disciplines and long birds at Sporting, but less useful for the close range targets of Skeet.

The pellets in any cartridge should be perfectly spherical and of a uniform size. Poor quality shot gives poor quality patterns, but generally manufacturers use excellent pellets in all their competition loads. Price is a big factor in the distribution of shotgun cartridges. Clayshooting accounts for a large slice of the volume sales in the UK and clayshooters tend to buy in bulk to reduce their overheads as much as possible. Since the abolition of Retail Price Maintenance the price of cartridges has risen very slowly and in 'real terms' cartridges are probably cheaper now than they have ever been.

The biggest change in cartridges has occurred in the last couple of years. This has been the change in the rules of many disciplines concerning the maximum permitted shot load. This change was led by the UIT (ISU). The shot loads for all the forms of shooting under their jurisdiction were reduced from 32g to 28g. The UK associations soon followed suit and since 1 January 1990 the majority of disciplines have been shot with the reduced load. The only exceptions are the FITASC disciplines and it is likely that Universal Trap will change in the near future. FITASC Sporting seems likely to remain at 36g for the foreseeable future.

This change has very little impact on shooters' scores. In the first year of international competition under UIT rules there has been virtually no reduction in the scores at major events. The 28g load has performed effectively, even on the second barrel shot at Olympic Trap. If it will cope successfully with the demands of Olympic Trap and Skeet, you need have no doubt about its effectiveness on any of the domestic disciplines. The only possible problem could be a psychological one. If you believe your scores will suffer because of the reduced load, then they probably will, but there is absolutely no practical reason for this to happen.

The introduction of the 28g load could lead to an upsurge of interest in the 20-gauge gun for clay target shooting. Major ammunition com-panies are already developing 28g loads for the 20-gauge which pattern as well as their 12-gauge equivalents. This could enable women and juniors to use a lighter gun without any unnecessary increase in recoil.

Generally, I think most shooters have settled down to the lighter load and find that their performances have not suffered. One of the benefits of the reduction in shot load has been a noticeable reduction in the level of sensible recoil, which is not only beneficial in medical terms, reducing the pounding that prolonged shooting gives the body, but it also helps gun control for the second shot. 28g loads are here to stay and after shooters have become used to them, few would wish to change back to the heavier loading.

Choosing a cartridge

The modern competition cartridge is loaded in a plastic case, with a plastic wad, hard shot (possibly nickel plated), a modern powder and sealed with a crimp closure. The majority of modern cartridges are more consistent in their performance than the majority of modern clayshooters. There are few if any really bad cartridges, but there are some very up-market high quality loadings available. These are loaded with the very best components and are generally more consistent ballistically. They are also considerably more expensive than the standard shell. At the top level of competition, the extra cost gives you a cartridge that might chip an extra target. That extra target might win you the competition, so it's a good idea to use the best available when it really counts.

Choice is largely a matter of experiment. Try a variety of different loads until you find one that suits your shooting and your pocket. Pattern them in your gun and practise with them at your chosen discipline. Once you have made a choice, stick with it so that you become used to that particular cartridge.

The storage of cartridges

This is an important point. While modern cartridges are extremely consistent and very stable under a wide variety of conditions, if you subject them to extremes of temperature problems can occur. I well remember the 1984 European Championships in Zaragoza. Ian Peel was suffering severe bruising to his face and shoulder during the competition. I found this most strange as we were both shooting the same shells (Fiocchi VIP3) and I was suffering no discomfort. Investigation soon revealed the cause. Ian had stored his shells in the boot of the hire car in the shooting ground car park. The Spanish sun was beating down on it. On opening the boot, I found that Ian's cartridges were hot to the touch. They had been slowly cooking inside the car with a consequent rise in chamber pressure

which resulted in a corresponding increase in recoil. Conversely, I once left a carton of cartridges overnight in the boot of the car in the depths of winter. At the shoot the next day I found that the cartridges appeared 'soft'. Inspection of the barrels revealed a considerable amount of unburnt powder. The freezing conditions overnight had reduced the performance of the shells.

The optimum conditions for cartridge storage are warm and dry, with a temperature around 60°F (15.5°C). Don't store them in the airing cupboard or alongside an Aga. Don't leave them in very cold conditions and if you are shooting in high temperatures, take steps to protect your shells. Don't leave them in the boot of the car unprotected. There are ABS cartridge boxes available on the market which are insulated and provide a measure of protection from extremes of temperature. Alternatively, one of those 'cool bags' or 'cool boxes' is ideal for keeping your cartridges in from the cold and out of the heat.

LEARNING TO SHOOT SUCCESSFULLY

The title of this chapter applies equally to beginners and those who have been shooting for years with little to show for it. This encompasses the vast majority of those who shoot registered competitions. Don't believe me? Get hold of a copy of the CPSA average book and browse through it. You'll notice that there are considerably more shooters in the lower classes than in AA (or A in the international disciplines), and many of these C and D class shooters have averages formulated over a large number of registered targets. They're doing plenty of shooting without getting anywhere. The reason for the preponderance of low classification clayshooters is that, despite the amount of targets they shoot, they have never learned to shoot effectively.

Gameshooters also often display the inadequacies of the self-taught shooter. Look at the photographs in shooting magazines of people in action at a game shoot. Most of them look awkward and off-balance because they have never learned a proper style of shooting. Added to this, they put in little or no practice in the off season. You soon realize why the

majority of gameshooters are inexorably bad shots, and in a sport which involves the killing of birds and animals, this reluctance to hone the shooting skills is indefensible.

The majority of people realize that they do not have an in-built ability to drive a car, play golf, ride a bike or acquire any number of other skills, yet so many of us think that we should be able to just pick up a gun and immediately be able to shoot without any formal instruction or guidance. There are some interesting comparisons with golf. A good set of golf clubs can cost as much as a reasonable shotgun. The man who spends a few hundred pounds on a set of clubs almost invariably goes along to the club professional to learn how to use them. The same man will spend a similar amount of money on a gun and it never enters his head to go to a shooting school and learn the basics from the outset. You will notice that I have referred to the male sex in this context: women seem to have no such inhibitions about seeking proper instruction, and indeed are generally much more receptive pupils at the shooting school. (Perhaps they don't have such fragile egos as the average male.)

So having established that most shooters have rather deficient levels of skill, how can they best improve, and how can the complete novice best begin? The simple answer is through proper coaching and a sound knowledge of the sport. By coaching I don't mean listening to the pearls of wisdom from the 'hotshot' at the local club. He may be a good shot but it doesn't follow that he is a good coach. We all know the situation where a shooter misses a target and his pals nod knowingly and tell each other 'He was behind that'. They then proceed to inform the hapless shooter when he comes off the line. This is not coaching. Even assuming the bystanders were correct in their analysis, the unfortunate shooter doesn't just want to know what he did wrong, he wants to know how to put it right! It's quite hilarious listening to a C class shooter telling a D class shooter where he's going wrong. If the C class shooter knows so much, how come he's not High Gun? The analysis and correction of faults in a shooter's style can be a complex business and is best left to a professional. A great deal can be gleaned from books like this one, but, without doubt, the best way to learn to shoot is to place yourself in the capable hands of an experienced coach. This will advance your shooting rapidly and the money is much better

Proper instruction at the start saves much frustration later on.

spent on lessons than wasting it on shooting mediocre scores in competitions.

A coach will instill the correct fundamentals into the beginner from the outset, but if you're already shooting, he has to eradicate your faults and replace them with a sound technique. To do this, he has to analyse every aspect of your style and technique, from how you stand to how you hold the gun.

The job of a coach is not just to identify your faults, but to correct them. In order for him to do this, you must approach the lessons in the right frame of mind. Firstly, the success, or otherwise, of the lesson is largely dependent on yourself. The instructor will endeavour to make the lesson interesting and informative, but he can't do the learning for you. You have to concentrate on making the lesson work for you. Make sure you understand the points the instructor is making. If you have any doubts, ask him to explain again. A good coach won't think you're stupid just because you don't grasp everything on the first telling. You must realize that the human mind can only learn a couple of things at a time and you must be realistic in what you expect to achieve from each lesson. Don't imagine that a session with a top instructor is going to make you into a World Champion overnight. A coach can only feed you information and tell you how to apply it. The application is entirely up to you. If your mind goes blank as you drive out of the shooting school gates, then you've wasted your money and the coach's time. All forms of teaching only guide you in the right direction: it is your responsibility to capitalize on the teaching and extract the maximum benefit from it. Learning is difficult, even for the brightest amongst us, but the old cliché is true, that the more you put in the more you'll get out.

It is important when having corrective coaching to shoot in your normal manner, because if you don't, it will be impossible for the coach to identify the real problem in your shooting. Likewise, don't try to impress the instructor—he's seen it all before and can probably shoot rings round you. You're not there to show off your brilliance, you are endeavouring to get your deficiences corrected!

During a lesson, it is important to remember how each new move feels when you perform it correctly. Much of shooting tuition is repetitive muscle/memory training. You are reprogramming the human computer to act instinctively, and, at the same time, learning to identify how and why you make mistakes. Don't worry if you miss a lot of targets so long as you are learning the right technique. Success comes as you start to perfect the new style.

A shooting lesson is not about breaking 100 per cent of the targets during instruction; it's all about learning in order to break 100 per cent Interchangeable stocks can quickly adapt an instructional gun for the smaller- or larger-framed novice.

of the targets during *competition*. Some years ago, a local game shooter visited the school in an attempt to improve his appalling shooting (his comment, not mine). During the course of a hundred clays he managed to hit about twenty of them. Naturally I was a little concerned about his lack of success, but the gentleman concerned wasn't worried. He said he could see what I was getting at and that I'd given him plenty to think about. That week-end he was to be a guest at a shoot in the Borders renowned for its high birds. First thing on Monday morning he was on the phone telling me how well he'd shot. He had given a great deal of thought to what I had been teaching him and had spent some time practising his gun-mounting, which was at the root of his problems. As a result he shot like a hero, hardly missing a bird all day. The moral here is that the lesson is only the beginning: it is up to you to use it as a starting point and develop accordingly. Remember the things you did right and concentrate on these so that you can duplicate them later in practice. You will often find with shooting that when you do it right, it also feels right. Concentrate on these points and lock them into your memory. Don't relax and let all the salient points fade from your mind as soon as you hit a few clays.

The lesson is the foundation of your shooting. Given the right foundation, it is up to you to build something worthwhile on it. After the lesson, review everything you've learned and commit it to memory. The next time you shoot without a coach, put it all into practice.

A WORD TO PARENTS

It is a natural thing for parents who are keen on a sport to want their children to become successful at it. When, on taking a child for lessons, it becomes apparent that he or she has talent, many a shooting father has got carried away, seeing a future Olympic Champion in the making. Please don't push a youngster hard because he or she shows signs of natural talent. Let them develop naturally otherwise you can destroy their enthusiasm for the sport. By all means encourage them to shoot, but let them enjoy it and remember that kids have a lot of other things to do in their lives. It is up to the child to make the decision about adopting a single-minded approach to the sport. Never make that decision for them, otherwise you'll find they will reject your favourite sport because they can't handle the pressure of a parent who expects too much of them. By all means back keen youngsters, but let them develop at their own pace. Don't drive them on, encourage them.

When encouraging a youngster to shoot, it pays to go to one good coach and stick to that one. Don't let well-meaning friends and fellow competitors offer advice, as much of it will be contradictory and confusion will set in rapidly.

THE
BASICS

Before dealing with the actual shooting we must take a look at safety. Generally speaking, clayshooting has a very good record on safety, much better than live quarry shooting. Part of this stems from the controlled atmosphere in which clayshooting is conducted but mostly it is a result of the vigilance of shoot organizers and shooting grounds.

It is impossible to be too cautious with a gun. Firearms were originally developed as weapons of war and by their very nature are inherently dangerous. They should **ALWAYS** be treated with a healthy respect for their destructive powers. Whatever form your shooting recreation takes, always be aware of safety.

There are a few basic rules that apply to all forms of shooting:

1. Treat every gun as if it were loaded. On picking up any sort of firearm, immediately check that it is unloaded by opening the action. Having ascertained that it is empty, keep the action open until you mean to use the gun.

2. Never put down any gun until you have checked that it is unloaded.

3. Never enter a building with a gun until you have checked that it is unloaded.

4. Never put your gun away at the end of shooting or on your return home until you have checked that it is unloaded.

5. NEVER, EVER, POINT A GUN AT ANYONE.

6. If you have any doubt about the safety of any part of your arc of fire, **DON'T** shoot. Always check first.

In general, accidents are not accidental, but are the result of carelessness.

There are a few specific safety rules that apply to all disciplines of clayshooting:

1. Never load your gun until you are situated on the relevant firing point.

2. If you gun misfires or malfunctions, keep it pointing downrange until the referee takes it from you to investigate the cause of the malfunction. **UNDER NO CIRCUMSTANCES SHOULD YOU TURN ROUND TOWARDS**

THE REFEREE. Failure to observe this rule resulted in one of the few fatalities to have afflicted our sport in the last fifty years.

3. When carrying your gun around at a shoot **ALWAYS** keep the action open until you are on the firing line and it is your turn to shoot. No one in the whole history of firearms has, to my knowledge, ever been shot by an open gun. Plenty of people have been shot with closed guns whose owners thought they were unloaded.

At the risk of labouring the point, check a gun when you pick it up, check it when you put it down, check it when you enter a vehicle or building, check it when you leave a vehicle or building, **CHECK IT, CHECK IT, CHECK IT**, and check it again. Better to be thought an 'old woman' than to be responsible for seriously, or fatally, injuring someone. Likewise, if you see someone else breaking safety rules, don't hesitate to remonstrate with them. If you neglect to tell them, they could go on to have an 'accident'. So, whoever they are, politely but firmly point out where their safety is deficient. Other people's lives depend on us all being safety conscious.

BASIC SHOOTING

In order to shoot successfully with a shotgun it is necessary to master certain fundamentals which form the basis for a sound shotgun technique, be it at game or clays. The very first thing a beginner must learn is that you do not aim a shotgun, you point it. The purpose of the little bead (foresight) on the end of the barrel is to make you subconsciously aware of the barrels. It is not there to enable you to aim the shotgun like a rifle. If you are looking at the foresight in order to align the gun you can't be looking at the clay moving across the sky, and if you are not looking at the clay you can't hit it! It is vitally important to realize this. The human eye cannot focus on a near object and a distant object at the same time, therefore focus on the variable: the moving target. A properly fitting and mounted gun will shoot where you look: all you have to do is look at the target and you have done most of the work required to hit it. This brings us on to gun fit and gun-mounting, two subjects which go hand in glove.

HOW TO HOLD THE GUN SO THAT IT SHOOTS WHERE YOU LOOK

Firstly, hold the gun by the grip with the muzzles pointing vertically.

Stand with your feet about eight inches apart. Now lean forward so that your weight is over the left foot. When moving into this position, make sure that the left hip remains straight. Some people find that the left hip tends to stick out when the weight is transferred to the left foot: if this happens it will cause loss of balance when moving after fast angle targets, so ensure that the left hip stays straight.

When the weight is shifted on to the left foot you may find that the right heel loses contact with the ground. This happens because the feet are too far apart. Bring the right foot forward just enough to enable the heel to regain contact with the ground. 70 per cent of your weight should now be over the left foot, but both feet should be in contact with the ground. When assuming this position make sure that the knees do not bend. The knees should be straight but not locked.

At this point you should find that your chin is over your left foot. Now raise your left hand to eye level and slightly bend your left elbow, and at the same time raise the gun until the heel of the stock is level with the right armpit. Lower the barrels until the forend is gripped by the left hand. Now, raise the stock to the right cheek, tilting the head forward, very slightly, to meet it. The gun should slip into the shoulder pocket and locate firmly. Do not pull the right shoulder back when it makes contact with the gun. At this stage your right eye should be looking directly along the rib and the gun will now shoot where you look. In this position, you and the gun have become one unit and your body and the gun must move together when reacting to a target. If your arms move the gun

faster than the rest of your body, then contact between the body and the gun will be lost, and the gun will no longer be pointing where your eyes are looking. A tiny loss of alignment at your end translates into a much greater error at the target.

This procedure establishes, at the outset, the correct placing of the gun in the shoulder pocket. You must perfect this positioning of the gun as it is a vital component of good gun-mounting. The correct alignment and balance of the gun and body provide the foundation on which good technique is built. Failure to locate the stock correctly leads to extensive bruising of the upper arm, something which is both painful and unnecessary.

THE DOMINANT EYE

At this stage, it is necessary to look at eye dominance or, as it is commonly known among shooters, the master eye. Obviously, eyesight controls the whole process of shooting, and the basic requirement of gun-mounting is to create a relationship between the eye and the gun that causes the gun to shoot where the vision is directed. In shotgun shooting the optimum is to shoot with both eyes open, as binocular vision gives us the best perception of distance and angle. To do this successfully, the eye looking directly along the barrel rib must provide the dominant visual signal to the brain.

To illustrate the difference between the two eyes, point the gun at a fixed mark and close the left eye. You will be looking directly along the barrel. However, if the right eye is closed, you will find that your vision is directed across the barrel and the gun would no longer shoot where you are looking. From this little experiment it becomes apparent that if you are right-handed and the left eye provides the dominant signal to the brain, then the point of impact of the shot charge will be significantly to the left of where your eyes are focused. This problem only manifests itself when shooting at a moving target, where there is no time to take deliberate aim. Rifle shooters do not suffer from this problem as their vision is chan-nelled by the sights along the barrel to the target, but, if you suffer from a mismatch between the dominant eye and the dominant hand, in the instinctive motion of shotgun shooting the sneaky mismatch of hand and eye will misdirect the gun barrels with disastrous consequences to your score.

There is a simple, reasonably effective test as to whether eye and hand dominance coincide. Stand with your right arm down at your side. Fix your vision, with both eyes open, on a fence-post about twenty yards away. Without shifting your vision, smartly raise the right arm and instinctively point at the post. Now close the left eye. If your hand and arm are still perfectly lined up with the post then your hand and eye dominance match, the dominant right hand is directed by a right master eye. However if, on closing the left

eye, the alignment of your arm to the post appears to move to the left of the post, then your left eye is the master and you have problems. Not insurmountable ones, but problems nevertheless.

At this point, it must be emphasized that eye dominance has absolutely nothing whatever to do with the strength of your eyes. It is quite possible for one eye to be much weaker than the other and yet still send the dominant signal to the brain. So don't think that an optician can sort out master eye problems for you. I have had a client at the shooting school whose sight in the right eye was very weak and steadily deteriorating towards blindness, and yet, with its greatly impaired vision, the right eye still retained dominance. If you have any doubts about eye dominance then the best course of action is to seek the help of a shooting school.

It is interesting that, whilst the majority of adult males have matching master eye/dominant hand, in many women there is a mismatch. Indeed, some women seem to have no definite master eye. When I first started coaching I was sometimes perplexed by women who appeared to have a dominant right eye one week but, on their return for the next lesson, seemed to have a left master eye. It was my good friend Paul Bentley, a coach of many years standing at the Holland & Holland shooting school, who put me right about this phenomenon. These observations about feminine eye dominance are not sexist, just a physiological fact of life!

So, if you have a problem with your master eye, what are you to do? Well, you are faced with a number of alternatives:

1. Change shoulders so that hand/eye dominance coincides.

2. Close the offending eye so that the correct eye can take over.

3. Have a cross-eyed stock fitted to your gun, enabling you to mount the gun to the right shoulder yet have the left eye looking down the barrels (or vice versa).

4. Continue to shoot abysmally.

We can discount option 4, assuming from the fact that you are reading this book that you want to improve your shooting.

Option 3, the cross-eyed stock, is not really a solution for anyone who aspires to be a serious and successful competition shooter. Under-and-over guns with cross-eyed stocks can be distinctly unpleasant to shoot with. The dog-leg configuration of the stock causes the gun to move about under recoil, making it hard to shoot effective second barrels; when firing large numbers of cartridges, the recoil can cause quite nasty facial bruising. Also it is difficult, although not impossible, to stock an under-and-over in this style because of the

bolt that runs through the hand of the stock.

This leaves options 1 and 2. As already said, binocular vision is best for shotgun shooting, so the best solution is to switch the gun to the same shoulder as the errant master eye. For a beginner this is undoubtedly the answer. If you are right-handed with a dominant left eye and have never shot before, it is only marginally more difficult to learn to shoot off the left shoulder.

Unfortunately, many people struggle with their shooting for some time before they discover they have a master eye problem. By this stage of the proceedings, much of the muscle training necessary to good shooting has become ingrained. This can make changing sides very difficult. If you are in this situation then closing the offending eye is the only option. This can take two forms: you can close the eye completely before calling for the target, making the one eye do all the work. This is the most appropriate solution for the Trap disciplines. Alternatively, you can call for the target with both eyes open and dim or half close the left eye as the muzzles move on to the target. This allows the right eye to take complete control of directing the gun as it is mounted.

THE GRIP

Naturally, your hands are one of the main points of contact between your

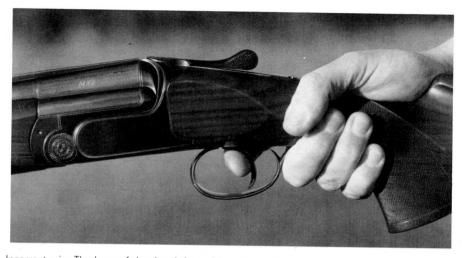

Incorrect grip. The base of the thumb is positioned too high over the grip, causing tension in the arm muscles which restricts free movement of the gun. The second finger is right up against the trigger guard which can result in a bruised knuckle.

gun and your body, and it is important that they hold the gun in a way that does not restrict your body's mobility. You must grip the gun in a manner that allows good control without putting unnecessary strain on any muscle groups. When muscles are placed under stress, their movement becomes restricted, and they act almost as a brake on your body. I see many beginners holding their guns in what amounts to a white-knuckle death grip. They look as if they are attempting to crush the gun's wood-work with their hands. This is usually prompted by fear of recoil. Amongst non-shooters there are awesome legends of the power of a shotgun's recoil, and many beginners believe that they will be hurled bodily

backwards at the instant of firing. This, of course is nonsense. If the gun is mounted and held correctly the body will naturally absorb the recoil, and the way you grip the gun makes an important contribution to this process.

THE RIGHT HAND

In addition to supporting the gun at the grip, this is the hand that pulls the trigger (if you are right-handed), therefore your hand must be positioned so that the index finger has proper control over the trigger. The part of the finger that should be in contact with the trigger blade is the pad. Do not use the first joint to operate the

Correct grip. Thumb and second finger meet around the stock giving optimum gun control. There is a gap between the second finger and trigger guard; the trigger is pulled with the pad of the index finger, rather than the joint.

trigger. Competition under-and-overs are fitted with single triggers. To function correctly, a single trigger mechanism requires that the shooter releases the trigger between the first and second shots. This is normally an involuntary action and the shooter is unaware that he does this. However, if the trigger is pulled with the first joint, it sometimes happens that the position of the finger inhibits this involuntary release of the trigger, preventing the action resetting itself for the second barrel. The gun will fail to fire the second shot, and, as this is not an allowable malfunction, you will lose the target. Therefore, use the pad of the index finger to pull the trigger. The pad is the most sensitive part of the finger, and is also the part that responds first when making a trigger-pulling motion. How you pull the trigger has a great effect on your timing, so strive for absolute consistency in finger/trigger placement.

Having established where the trigger finger is located, take hold of the pistol grip, curling the thumb around the grip so that it meets the tip of the middle finger. A firm grip with the thumb and second, third and fourth fingers should provide complete gun control whilst leaving the trigger finger relaxed and responsive. If the trigger finger is under tension, your timing will suffer, and in extreme cases you can find it impossible to fire the gun.

There are three things to be aware of about the right hand. Firstly, be

Another incorrect grip. If the gun slips under recoil there is a good chance that the thumb will be split open by the top lever.

sure to leave a space between the trigger guard and the middle finger: failure to do this can cause bruising under recoil as the knuckle of the middle finger makes contact with the guard. Using the joint to pull the trigger aggravates this problem, so remember to use the pad.

Secondly, watch for any tendency for the web of the right hand to ride up on to the top of the grip as this can inhibit the vertical swing of the gun.

Finally, make sure you wrap your thumb around the grip—**NEVER** leave it lying along the top as this leaves it vulnerable to being hit by the top lever. This is extremely painful and the sharp edge of the lever can easily split the thumb.

THE LEFT HAND

The left hand and arm act rather like the steering on a car. Their function is to control the pointing of the gun at the target. To do this efficiently, the left hand grip must not produce unnecessary tension in the left arm. An incorrect grip with the left hand tightens the muscles in the left arm and causes opposing muscle groups to pull against each other. This inhibits smoothness and often causes a jerky swing as the body fights against itself. Additionally, this muscle tension soon leads to fatigue during a big competition.

You should, initially, grip the forend as far out as you can *comfortably* reach whilst still keeping the left elbow broken. The location of the left

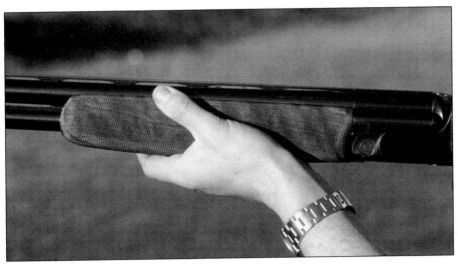

Incorrect forend grip. Here the hand is positioned under the forend inducing tension in the arm muscles. A gun held in this position moves vertically initially as the shooter responds to the target.

Correct forend grip. The gun lies in the hand and the arm responds to varying trajectories much more easily.

It is important for beginners to be taught how to hold the gun correctly right from the outset.

hand on the forend can be modified in the light of experience, remembering that moving the hand back towards the action speeds up the momentum of the swing due to increased leverage, but at the same time control diminishes. Conversely, locating the hand further forward gives better control, but restricts the swing. In time you will discover the ideal position, but be prepared to adapt it to suit exceptionally slow or fast targets.

The left hand forms a channel for the gun to sit in. The palm should be located along the side of the forend, the bottom of the forend sitting in a cradle made by the fingers. The left index finger may be pointed along the forend on a line level, or just below, the centre rib of the barrels. The gun should now be resting on the middle finger. A moderate grip with the hand in this position should provide positive gun control without tensing the arm muscles. Do not hold the forend so that the bottom is sitting in the palm. This not only strains the muscles in the forearm, but also makes your initial gun movement vertical, regardless of the trajectory of the target. This is a disadvantage on low or crossing targets.

Both hands and arms help the body absorb recoil and correct placing of the hands considerably reduces the amount of sensible recoil felt by the shoulder.

GUN-MOUNTING

Correct and consistent gun-mounting is essential to good shooting.

Having established the correct placement of the gun in the shoulder, and how to hold it, the next step is to learn how to mount it from a 'gundown' position.

First, adopt the foot position described earlier. The gun is then positioned so that the heel of the stock is placed under the armpit. The left hand is elevated so that the muzzle of the gun is at eye level. Line up the muzzles and the eyes with a fixed point at about head height. Push the gun towards this fixed point with the left hand, making sure that the muzzles stay in line with it. As you push the gun forward the stock slips out from under the armpit, and the butt slides up the body into the shoulder pocket. As the butt comes into the shoulder pocket, the right shoulder hunches forward as if it was about to push against a heavy weight. This places the gun correctly and firmly in the shoulder and enables your body to absorb recoil. It is important that the gun is held firmly against the shoulder but guard against any undue tension. This will ensure that the recoil pushes against you, and you and the gun move together as one unit. If the gun is held loosely, then the result is painful: the gun moves under recoil, hits you, which hurts, and *then* your body moves.

As the butt slides into the shoulder, the face makes contact with the side of the stock and the comb of the stock comes to rest against under the cheek-bone. Throughout this procedure the muzzles remain firmly locked on to the fixed point.

Practise the above procedure until the gun slides easily into the shoulder without the muzzles wavering from your line of sight. Use a mirror to check that the gun is properly aligned. The pupil should appear just above, and central to, the rib.

Once you have perfected the above procedure it is time to introduce simulated target flight into the equation. This is easily done by using a horizontal line, such as a telephone line or the top of a wall, to swing along whilst mounting the gun. The muzzles are placed on the line and

Incorrect stance. There is no relationship between the shooter's eyes, the gun muzzles and the point where the target emerges.

Incorrect stance. Here the shooter is looking across the side of the gun and the barrels need to be pulled across and down during mounting to bring them into the line of sight. This excessive movement causes inconsistent and inaccurate gun mounting and wastes time.

the left hand pushes the barrels along the line as you mount the gun using the procedure outlined above.

When practising this, concentrate on the following:

1. Keep the eyes focused on the horizontal line. Imagine it is the flight of a target.

2. Strive to make the actual mounting of the gun as smooth and as solid as possible.

3. Remember to use the left hand to direct the gun.

4. Start practising slowly at first, concentrating on perfecting the technique. As the movements become more comfortable, you will find things will speed up naturally.

44

Incorrect stance. The body weight is centred over the back foot which gives poor balance. Again there is no eye/gun muzzle relationship and the gun must be 'cartwheeled' during mounting to bring the muzzles down to the line of sight.

A good ready position. Body weight is well distributed with a bias on the front foot. The eyes and the muzzles are lined up ready to move on the target. The shooter looks alert and responsive.

5. Don't overdo it when practising this. Five to ten minutes at a time is enough, as your arms will become tired and concentration will flag. A little and often is the maxim.

* It goes without saying that you practise the foregoing with an un-loaded gun, in a secluded location!

This type of 'dry' training, if carried out conscientiously, should soon have you mounting the gun correctly and consistently. You will then be able to tackle moving targets with confidence. One of the problems with beginners is a tendency to rush everything when confronted with a moving clay. Their brain is trying to concentrate on the clay and direct gun-mounting operations at the same time. In consequence their concentration is divided, and panic sets in causing the gun to make contact with the body anywhere but in the right place! This leads to missed clays and bruises! However, if you have confidence in your gun-mounting before tackling moving targets, your brain can concentrate on the important thing, the trajectory and speed of the clay. When gun-mounting becomes second nature, you will discover you have far more time than you ever thought.

All of the above might sound a little tedious to the beginner anxious to join battle with the real thing, but it is very important, especially in the early part of your shooting career. Time spent perfecting technique is never wasted and it can save you a lot of time and money in attaining a reasonable standard. I remember a ten-year-old pupil at the shooting school who was shown how to practise the above technique as 'homework' between lessons. He practised with an air rifle, under the supervision of his father, for a few minutes every day. When he returned to the school for the next lesson, his shooting improved beyond recognition and he made rapid progress towards becoming a very good shot indeed.

STARTING TO SHOOT

When the big moment comes and you are standing there waiting for your first target to appear, your mind will be spinning with all the theory you have been assimilating. Relax — you're meant to be doing this for enjoyment!

Through constant dry practice, your stance and gun-mounting should give you no cause for worry. A few shots at a pattern plate will have made you familiar with the sensation of a gun going off. The only new element that has crept into the picture is the moving clay target. As the clay represents the unknown, your concentration should be focused on seeing it the moment it appears. This means looking for it. This sounds rather obvious but it is amazing how many newcomers to the sport don't look for the target. Most make the mistake of looking at their guns. How they expect to see something 20 yards away when their eyes are focused 30 inches away beats me. You will not make that mistake. Having complete confidence that your gun-mounting will ensure your gun will point where you are looking, you will concentrate your eyes on seeing the target as soon as is humanly possible. As the target appears, your vision must 'lock on' to it to the exclusion of everything else. As the golfer keeps his eye on the ball, so you must keep yours on the target. Do not be tempted to look at the gun barrels; when your eye is allowed to look away from the target you lose contact with it. I cannot overemphasize this need to keep your eye on the target: it is the brain's response to accurate visual stimulus that directs the body to perform a successful shot. Your visual response to the clay is the spark that fires up the motor. If it's crisp and positive, you fire up straight-away, if it's sluggish and hesitant, you tick over before starting to respond. So concentrate and look!

For the beginner, there is an added benefit to this intense concentration on the target. When your brain is tied up with identifying and hitting that clay, you don't notice the noise and commotion of the gun going off. Most beginners are apprehensive about the first few shots in anger, but if you concentrate on the important things, this apprehension will soon disappear.

THE TARGET

Some instructors start beginners off on a simple going away target. I feel this is a mistake as it encourages deliberate aiming, something that must be avoided from the outset. My own preference is to use an incoming target about 20-30 feet high.

Adopt the position described earlier, with the stock tucked under the armpit. Point the muzzles of the gun slightly ahead of where you first expect to see the target. As the target appears, the eyes lock on to it. As it comes to the muzzles of the gun, the left hand starts the gun moving so that the muzzles join the eyes in being locked on to the target. As the left hand moves forward on to the target the rest of the body moves with it, allowing contact with the clay to be maintained. As the stock slips into the shoulder and the gun is properly mounted, the muzzles accelerate away from the target and the

trigger is pulled, resulting in a satisfying destruction of the clay.

It is important to continue the gun movement after the shot is fired. This follow through eliminates any tendency to stop the gun at the instant of firing. The other important thing to remember is to keep the head firmly in contact with the stock until well after the shot has been fired. There is a terrible temptation to lift the head to see the result of your shot. This means your eyes and your gun have strayed apart and the gun will no longer shoot where you are looking. Disastrous!

Remember the gun-mounting instruction and make sure that the muzzles move first. Many shooters raise the stock to their shoulders before moving the muzzles after the clay, totally destroying any relationship between the target and the gun. If you are not convinced about this, try a little experiment. Hold the gun in the ready position, as if you were about to call for a target. Now raise the stock to the face without moving the left hand. As the stock comes up the muzzles will move down. You want those muzzles to lock on to the flightline of targets, rather than moving down and away from them. If you raise the stock to the face before moving the muzzles, you will always be struggling to establish contact between the gun and target.

You should practise on this incoming target until you can hit it time after time. When you reach this stage, move in towards the trap. This

47

will make the target a little faster and will speed up your gun-mounting and reactions. By progressing slowly at this stage you are reinforcing everything you learn and laying the foundations for future good shooting. One thing that will soon become apparent is that when the shot *feels* good the result *is* good, when it feels rushed and awkward you usually miss. Strive for that harmony and co-ordination right from the start — it's far more important than speed in the early stages. When your gun-handling becomes more confident, speed will naturally follow.

CROSSING TARGETS

The important point to establish when tackling crossing targets is that everyone has what one shooting coach describes as an 'easy swing' area. It usually equates to an area about 60° either side of centre. Within this part of your swing the body moves freely in either direction but outside of it, your muscles run out of stretch and your swing inevitably starts to slow down. When shooting crossing targets it is essential that both the targets be engaged within this 'easy swing' section.

You use the same basic technique to shoot this target, except that now the gun is moving in the horizontal plane instead of the vertical. The eyes lock on to the target as it appears, the left hand directs the muzzles on to the clay, the gun is

mounted as the body pivots on the left foot, the muzzles accelerate away from the clay and the trigger is pulled.

FORWARD ALLOWANCE

On crossing targets the amount of apparent lead, or forward allowance, will vary from shooter to shooter depending on how fast they accelerate the gun. If your gun-mounting is sound, you can move the gun much faster and thus see less lead. In fact it is possible to move the gun at a speed that makes it appear that you are firing directly at the clay. In order to exploit this technique your gun-mounting must be faultless: time spent practising and perfecting your gun-mounting is never wasted. Indeed, dry practice is a very effective and cheap way of improving your shooting. Poor gun-mounting is probably the most common cause of missed targets, whatever the discipline you are shooting. If the gun-mount is incorrect everything following it will be incorrect. This applies equally to gun-up and gun-down disciplines. There is no excuse for poor gun-mounting, particularly at Trap disciplines, and if you have problems in this area you must take all possible steps to correct them.

If you cannot put your finger on the problem, seek help from an experienced coach. The money invested in coaching will save you a fortune in wasted cartridges.

GUN FIT

Perhaps this should be subtitled 'shooter fitting' because the vast majority of clay shooters fit themselves to the gun rather than having the gun fitted to the shooter.

Most champion shooters, however, either have their guns altered to fit or they experiment with different guns until they find one that does fit.

I suppose the definition of a properly fitted gun would be one with stock dimensions, and handling characteristics, that enable the shooter to fully exploit his natural hand/eye coordination. Notice that I include handling in this. A gun with the most perfect set of stock dimensions would be useless if ill-balanced or of a weight unsuitable for the shooter's physique. It must be emphasized that gun fit relates not just to a shooter's physical dimensions but also to his style and discipline of shooting. It is impossible to fit a gun just by measuring up the shooter. This might produce a well-fitted suit of clothes but it is only a part of gun fitting. At this point it should be stated that the only reliable way to get properly fitted is to visit a qualified gun fitter at a good shooting school. The school can then correct faults in shooting technique before fitting, rather than attempting to alter the gun to compensate for the shooter's failings. It is possible for the individual to fit a gun to himself by trial and error but going to a good shooting school saves an awful lot of time and frustration.

SPORTING SHOOTING

Sporting, in its various guises, is without doubt the most popular of all the forms of clayshooting. The vast majority of people will start their clayshooting careers on Sporting targets. Part of its popularity is due to the fact that Sporting forms the link between game shooting and clay target shooting, and many shooters who have no desire to compete at clay targets use Sporting clays as practice for live game. The better shooting grounds design layouts that go a long way towards simulating the kind of shots that a game shooter would encounter in the field. In this sense Sporting is the oldest discipline.

However, in the last twenty years there has been a huge expansion in the shooting of competitive Sporting clays and nowadays there are quite a few top Sporting shooters who never fire a shot at live game. It is no longer just practice for game shooting: Sporting has become a serious competitive sport at both domestic and international level. At international level, Great Britain must rank as the most successful nation currently taking part. This country has produced many World and European Champions, and we have a record in the sport that all shooters, whatever their discipline,

should be very proud of.

There are two distinct variations of competitive Sporting clays shot in Britain. The first, and by far the most popular, is English Sporting, so called because it is governed by the rules of the English CPSA. The international, and more demanding, form is known as FITASC Sporting or Parcours de Chasse. This, as its title suggests, is governed by the rules of FITASC.

ENGLISH SPORTING

As a discipline, English Sporting has probably seen more changes in the last twenty years, than any other form of clayshooting. Although the basic format has remained the same, different types of clay target have become available and shoot organizers have shown increasing imagination in the way they present them.

When I first started shooting Sporting in the 1960s, the targets at all Sporting shoots were fairly predictable and it was very rare to see anything other than standard clays, invariably black, being thrown. Minis, midis (90mm) and battues were unheard of. There were only a couple of trap manufacturers and consequently there was quite a severe limit to the variation in target speed that could be obtained.

Things have really changed in the last few years. There are now a huge number of different traps available, all with different throwing characteristics, which enable shooting grounds to present an infinite variety of speeds and angles. Additionally, the English CPSA has modified its rules to allow other types of clays, such as battues and minis, to be used. Unfortunately, they only allow a maximum of 30 per cent non-standard clays but even that helps make the sport more interesting. These changes, in traps, targets and the rules have given organizers much greater scope in designing imaginative and challenging courses and have given the sport a real boost.

The format of an English Sporting layout is very straightforward. There will be a number of different stands which can be shot in any order. On each stand the competitor will shoot at three to five pairs depending on whether it is a 30, 50 or 100 bird competition. Single targets are rarely thrown in major competitions but may be encountered in the more informal shoots or at local gun clubs. Pairs come in three varieties: simultaneous pairs where the targets are released together; following pairs where the second target follows the first with very little delay; and report pairs where the second clay is released at the sound of the competitor's shot at the first clay.

THE SPORTING GUN

In the 1960s the typical sporting shooter usually carried at least two guns around a layout, normally a Skeet gun for the bulk of the targets, and a Trap gun for the long range targets. Some shooters opted for a game gun as a compromise, but as game guns tend to be lighter in weight, recoil punishment could be a problem in the bigger shoots. Although Sporting was growing in popularity, the gun manufacturers didn't take it seriously and obviously felt there was no need for a specialist Sporting gun. Browning did go some way towards meeting the demand by offering their B25 Skeet gun with the option of much tighter choking, but it still resembled a Skeet gun and handled like one. The modern Sporting gun had yet to evolve.

Nowadays nearly every major gun manufacturer offers Sporting models and the majority of these owe their design to the ideas of a top British shooter. In the 1970s Brian Hebditch was (and still is) one of Britain's finest Sporting shots. He used a Browning Skeet model, with the optional tighter chokes, to great effect, winning many major events including the European Championship. Although successful with the gun, Brian felt the handling of the gun was not helped by the bulky beavertail forend. At the time Brian was a gamekeeper and obviously saw a lot of different game guns, including Brownings. One day he had the brilliant idea of taking the slim schnabel forend off a Browning Lightweight Game gun and fitting it to his choked Skeet gun in place of the factory forend. This transformed the gun, reducing the overall weight and making it far more pointable.

I first saw this gun at a Sporting shoot at Cheddar Valley Gun Club and, like most shooters seeing something new, asked if I could have a shot with it. I used it on the most difficult stand on the course and shot far better than I expected. It handled so much better than guns fitted with the usual bulky, beavertail forends. I really liked the gun, and fortunately for today's Sporting shooters, so did Browning. On seeing Brian's 'prototype' they saw its advantages and put it into production as the Model 205 Special Sporting. This was soon followed by the Model 206 which had 30in barrels for the shooter who liked a long gun. Thus the modern Sporting clay gun was born. For a few years Browning dominated the market, but then the other manufacturers caught up. Today, Brian Hebditch is part of the Gunmark team, and has been responsible for much of the development of Beretta's excellent range of Sporting clay guns.

So, after that little bit of history, what is the ideal Sporting clay gun? Well, there is a much greater variation in target angles, speeds and distances in Sporting than in any other discipline. Therefore you require a gun that can cope with all these variations. To do this successfully, I believe that the gun should have stock dimensions that make it easy to mount and that cause it to shoot where you look. There has been a fashion lately for Sporting guns with higher stocks, but for every top shooter who uses a high stock there will be ten who perform better with a flat shooting gun. As an example, a high Trap stock would make shooting a steeply rising 'teal' much easier due to its higher point of impact. However, such a gun would be a liability on a close, fast, 'bolting bunny' where a quick, instinctive shot is required.

There is no one specification that will enable all and sundry to cope with all these variations effectively. The best answer is to take yourself along to a reputable clayshooting specialist in the gun trade and handle a selection of different Sporting models by a variety of manufacturers. If you feel you don't have the experience to make the choice, put yourself in the hands of a professional coach and let him see you shoot. This should enable him to advise you as to a suitable gun. There are certain characteristics that all good Sporting guns possess. These are all related to handling. A good Sporting gun will generally have a slim forend, lighter barrels than would be found on a Trap gun of similar barrel length, and a point of balance on the hinge pin or just forward of it. This all makes for a lively, easy handling, pointable gun. For those who like something a little steadier, try longer barrels — 30in or even 32in.

THE SIDE-BY-SIDE

In the very early days of Sporting competition, virtually everyone used side-by-side game guns. As the under-and-over became more wide-spread, the side-by-side disappeared from the list of prizewinners. By the 1960s the majority of top Sporting shooters were using under-and-overs or semi-automatics. Only 'fun shooters' still used the side-by-side. Recently this has changed as sponsors have sought to encourage the 'grass roots' shooters to take part in major championships. Most of the big Sporting shoots now have prizes exclusively for side-by-side users. This has led to a renewed interest in the side-by-side as a competition gun. Although many taking part in this category use standard game guns, there are a few specialized side-by-sides available that are more suitable to the rigours of regular competitive use.

These guns are generally a fair bit heavier than game guns, and thus have less sensible recoil using competition cartridges. Usually they have single selective triggers combined with pistol grip stocks and some even have raised ventilated ribs. This makes for handling qualities more akin to an under-and-over than a side-by-side game gun. Two such guns are the 626 Beretta and the Winchester Model 23. Either of these guns would be an excellent choice for the shooter making a serious attack on the side-by-side prize list.

INTERCHANGEABLE CHOKES

These are a recent development in under-and-overs. First produced in the mid-1970s by Perazzi on their MT6 model, the idea was soon taken up by Winchester. It proved immensely popular and most of the other major manufacturers followed suit. Although I own a number of guns with screw-in chokes I am a little dubious as to their advantages. To exploit inter-changeable chokes fully it is necessary to pattern your gun with every choke you have for it. It is also too easy to blame a miss on a poor choice of choke rather than on bad shooting. Herein lies the road to ruin — shooters spend more time worrying about their chokes than thinking about the targets they have to shoot. The best advice I can give is to install ¼ choke in both barrels and only alter it in exceptional circumstances. In a fixed choke gun, ¼/¼ or ¼/½ should prove the ideal combination.

TECHNIQUE

Sporting is the one discipline where all the recognized styles of shotgun shooting can be used successfully. Indeed, many top Sporting shots will admit to varying their technique according to the type of target on a particular stand. On some stands they 'swing through', on others they shoot with maintained lead, and on some they let the acceleration of the gun do all the work for them. Probably the best way to explain Sporting is to go through the various types of targets presented and discuss how to deal with them.

TARGET IDENTIFICATION

Before tackling any stand on a Sporting layout you must identify the targets being used. Now that the CPSA allows up to 30 per cent non-standard clays there is a good chance you will come up against minis, midis, battues and rabbits at an English Sporting shoot. At the big competitions you will probably notice the top shooters 'walking' the course before they start to shoot. This is good policy as it enables you to plan the order in which to shoot the stands. At the same time you can identify the non-standard targets and the tricky stands. Shoot organizers are more devious these days, so look at each target very carefully as they are not always what they seem. For instance, at a recent CPSA selection shoot on my own ground, I threw a normal black clay from a rabbit trap. This was presented to the shooter as a driven target, curling in an arc towards the stand. The majority of competitors thought this target was a battue. This caused many of them to completely misread its speed with disastrous consequences! By mixing clay types and traps it is possible to produce some really deceiving targets, so read them carefully.

DRIVEN

Nearly every big Sporting competition will have at least one driven stand, many will have two or three with targets presented at differing heights and angles. The most basic driven target is the medium height, simultaneous, 'head on' pair, often referred to as a 'Driven Partridge' or 'Driven Grouse'. Often these clays are on top of the shooter very quickly so there is no time to hang about. The first thing you must decide, with any simultaneous pair, is which of the two targets you are going to shoot first. This is where a little time spent studying the targets can pay dividends. Well before your turn to shoot you should be watching carefully as other competitors shoot this stand. Watch the targets, not how the other shooters are doing it. After all, they might be getting it wrong! The easy answer as to which target to take first is that you should shoot at the one which catches your eye first. This is a good general rule but like all generalities often needs to be modified in specific circumstances. If one of the pair is flying to the left or right of the shooter, with the other target 'head on', then normally you should take the straighter target first. The 'head on' target is relatively easy if

This 'ready' position for sporting. Eyes and muzzles lined up. Stock touching the body below the armpit. An ideal stance for English or FITASC sporting.

taken out in front, but, as it is closing on you, the later you leave it the harder it becomes.

There is an exception to this rule, however: close driven battues. Some layout designers have discovered that it is possible to throw a particularly evil pair by using a trap with a standard arm and placing one battue upside down. This gives a peculiar twisting target out to one side. This is best shot first and quickly, before it has time to turn edge on, leaving the straighter target as the second shot.

After careful observation, you have decided the order in which you are going to shoot the pair. Watch the shooters in front of you and determine exactly where the targets are coming from and the earliest point your eyes can pick them up. Now it's your turn to shoot. Adopt a ready position which enables you to shoot the first target quickly and positively, but that also allows enough freedom of move-ment, within the confines of any cage, to cover the second clay without undue contortion. Place the muzzles slightly above the 'visual pick-up point'. Concentrate on seeing that first target as quickly as possible. Now call for the targets.

As the targets appear, a number of things should happen simultaneously. Your eyes lock on to your chosen 'first bird'. Your body weight shifts slightly forward over the front foot. Your left hand (in the case of right-handed shooters) starts pushing out towards the target and moves the muzzles in concert with the 'first bird'

and your 'locked-on' vision. You should see the target on the end of the gun. As the left hand and the eyes lock in, the right hand is allowing the stock to slide into the shoulder. Do not lift with the right hand as this will cause the muzzles to dip, causing them, and your eyes, to come off the line of flight. The result of this is your gun is mounted but nowhere near the chosen target, leaving you chasing all over the sky to regain contact, and wasting precious time. This causes both shots to be taken in a panic-stricken rush with disastrous consequences for your scorecard. So remember, direct the gun with the left hand and keep the muzzles and your eyes 'locked on' to the target.

As the stock makes contact with the face and shoulder, the muzzles accelerate through the target and the trigger is pulled. The swing is maintained for a split second as the muzzles follow through. The speed of the swing takes care of lead and keeps the whole procedure sharp and crisp. Keep the body weight over the front foot at all times. Any tendency to shift on to the back foot will cause loss of balance, and drags the muzzles and vision away from the target.

Whilst engaging the first target, your attention should have been focused on it 100 per cent. Having delivered the first shot, now is the time to switch to the second bird. How you deal with this rather depends on how close it is to the first. If the pair of clays are close together on the same line, then let your eyes find the second target and lock on to it. The left hand (and muzzles) follow the eyes, the gun accelerates through the target and the shot is taken. Easy. Unfortunately, in many instances the line of the second target will differ from that of the first even when the clays are presented from the same trap. In these circumstances, the gun is dropped slightly out of the shoulder as the eyes locate the second target. As everything locks on again the gun slides back into the shoulder and as it accelerates through the target the trigger is pulled. As with the first target, and for the same reasons, keep your weight over the front foot. It is very easy to let the weight shift as you move on to the second bird. This will cause slight loss of balance with dire consequences to smoothness and gun control. At all times when shotgun shooting strive to be as smooth as possible in your body movements. This is very important: if you concentrate on smoothness, speed will come naturally.

You will notice that I have said little about lead. This is because I prefer to shoot with a rapidly accelerating gun which cuts down apparent lead. I find that on close driven targets all that is required is to 'blot out' the target as the gun accelerates through it and maintain the swing for that split second after pulling the trigger. Thus the shot becomes almost instinctive. I have found, particularly with beginners, that people's instinctive actions are generally more effective than their deliberate ones. Naturally, instinctive shooting relies heavily on very good gun-mounting but then all shotgun shooting depends on this and beginners would do well to spend time on perfecting their gun-mounting rather than computing leads.

GOING AWAY TARGETS

The straight going away target should present few problems, provided you resist the temptation to aim at it. It is very tempting, with the clay seeming to hang in the air in front of you, to try to line up the foresight on target. This is fatal. You must always focus on the target: don't let your eyes stray to the gun. It is important to attack going away targets, don't attempt to ride them out, as this gives you more time in which to make an error.

Observe the flightline whilst the previous shooters are in action. This should enable you to judge the height and speed of the target. Set yourself up so that you are facing along the path of the clay's flight. Hold the gun so that it points along the flightpath with the muzzles a fraction below the point where you can first see the target. The bodyweight should be evenly distributed across the feet but as the target appears, and the gun-mounting begins, the weight shifts on to the front foot. As the body moves, the left hand pushes out, keeping the muzzles locked on to the target, and the stock slides smoothly into the shoulder. As the gun beds into the shoulder the trigger is pulled. These movements shouldn't be rushed, but should be accomplished positively and without hesitation. The target must be attacked but you must remain in total control. If you rush, your gun-mounting will become erratic and the muzzles will veer off the clay's flightline. If this occurs you will be trying to realign the gun at the moment you should be pulling the trigger.

Going Away Pairs

The important thing to remember here is that you can't kill a pair if you miss the first target. This sounds rather obvious but it is surprising how many shooters seem to want to look at both targets at the same time! Before entering the stand you should have decided which target you are going to take first. Shoot the first bird exactly as described above. Having killed it, your eyes switch to the second target. As the eyes move the left hand is pulling the gun down out of recoil. The left hand pushes the muzzles on to the line of the second bird and as they reach the target the trigger is pulled. On close receding doubles there is no need to partially dismount the gun whilst switching targets. I know that conventional teaching urges this remounting of the gun between shots, but I see little need for it on straight away doubles.

Double Rise DTL shooters don't remount between shots and there is no need for Sporting shooters to do it on this type of target. You know where the second target is going, so be positive and don't waste time.

The situation changes if the second bird of the pair takes a completely different trajectory to the first. Then you must treat the double as two separate singles. Shoot the straighter of the pair first, drop the gun slightly out of the shoulder, push the muzzles onto the second target with the left hand, at the same time remounting the gun, pulling the trigger as the muzzles sweep through the second target.

SPRINGING TEAL

One of the classic Sporting stands, the clays represent the near vertical take-off of startled teal. 'Springing' is the perfect adjective to describe the flight of the real bird and most shooting grounds do a good job of emulating this with clays. Usually the teal stand consists of a sharply rising pair of targets which rise simultaneously from a concealed trap anything from five to thirty yards in front of the shooter. Although it is a simultaneous pair it is important to treat these as two entirely separate targets.

Before entering the stand your observation of the targets will have helped you decide which you are going to take first. The first target must be shot on the rise, approximately half-way to the apex of its flight. At this point in its flight it is still moving very rapidly so there is no time to waste. The shot must be taken swiftly and positively. In order to do this your gun-mounting must be spot on, emphasizing again the need to practise gun-mounting. Perfecting it is absolutely essential to success in all disciplines.

Point the gun about half-way between the trap and where you intend to break the target. As the bird appears the muzzles are swung up the flightline as the gun is mounted. When the muzzles overtake the target, the shot is fired with the gun still accelerating. You must not stop the gun as you fire, as this will guarantee a miss behind. It is necessary to attack this first target and maintain your swing as you pull the trigger. It is most important that you stick to your chosen first target. Ignore the second until you have dealt with the first. If you try to focus on both targets, your swing will lose momentum, causing hesitation, usually followed by a panic-stricken stab at one of the targets, resulting in a miss, unless you are very lucky. Remember, pick a target and concentrate on it until it's shot.

Having massacred the first bird you turn to the second. This is where the problems can occur. Your first shot was taken relatively quickly at a rapidly climbing target. By the time you have made that first shot the second target will be reaching the top of its flight. Gravity will be causing it to decelerate, prior to falling back to earth. This second target is a totally different shot to the first. Having delivered the first shot, the stock is allowed to break contact with the shoulder as the left hand directs the muzzles on to the second target. As the gun is remounted the shot is fired directly at the clay. Make this second shot as soon as the muzzles reach the target, any hesitation in an attempt to 'make sure' will leave you shooting at a dropping, sliding target — definitely something to avoid.

Normally, Springing Teal are pretty straightforward, the speed of the target and the distance from the shooter being the two variables which determine the degree of difficulty. Sometimes, though, you may come across 'something completely different'. Such a stand is the Springing Teal at Falkirk Gun Club in Central Scotland. Some evil-minded committee member had the idea of situating the Teal trap at the top of a bank about twenty-five yards in front of the shooter. Thus, you are confronted with a target that is starting out higher than most teal targets fly! If you come across something like this, don't panic. The technique remains the same, just move the muzzles up to cover the line of flight, and shoot exactly the same as if the target was coming from ground level. These odd stands are usually designed to frighten you into missing targets. If you keep your head, watch carefully, and maintain your technique, you should have no problems. So much of successful shooting is about having confidence in your own ability to read targets correctly. If you let doubts creep in, you are lost.

DROPPING DUCK

This is the generic term for targets thrown from behind the stand over the shooter's head. Usually the shooter is caged in such a way that it is impossible to turn to face the trap, thus making it necessary to shoot the clays after they have passed over the shooter's head. This introduces another variable into the target's flight because, not only is it going away, but it is also dropping. Targets presented in this manner from a low trap should give few problems: they are dealt with in exactly the same way as Station 1 Skeet. The problems start when the clays are thrown from a tower or similar high point as this can exaggerate the dropping effect of the trajectory.

There are two techniques that can be applied to this particular target. The one common feature of both methods is not to let the targets get ahead of the gun as this will require an exaggerated swing downwards to catch up with the target, let alone get ahead of it.

The conventional method is to start with the muzzles well up, looking straight up above, or slightly behind you. The weight is centred

over the front foot and the back arched. It looks uncomfortable but it enables you to see the target early. If you look out in front you will guarantee that the clay has passed your gun before you can react to it, leaving you racing uncontrollably after it. So, look as far behind as your arched back will allow. As the target comes into view the muzzles start to move ahead of it. To maintain this movement it should be obvious that the muzzles must drop as the swing continues. For this reason it is advantageous to let the right hand do more work in mounting the gun. Normally the left hand leads and the right hand follows, but with this particular target you require the muzzles to drop to stay on the line of flight so let the right hand do more work in the initial stages of mounting.

As the target appears, the muzzles move down and ahead of the target, maintaining this position in front of the target until the required lead is registered and the shot fired. When the first target has been dealt with, the gun moves across on to the line of the second target and ahead of it. Once again the shot is delivered as

The ready position for pairs from behind. The conventional way: the body leans back to see the target as early as possible.
Note: In this, and the subsequent photograph, the safety cage has been removed for clarity. These types of targets should always be shot from an enclosed (3 sides) safety cage.

60

soon as the required lead is registered. As this method is basically 'maintained lead' you will be aware of much greater apparent lead than normal.

My own preferred method for shooting these targets is rather different and certainly unconventional. I prefer to treat the first target as a high crosser, shooting it as near the vertical as possible, then slightly turning the upper torso to shoot the second bird as a going away before it starts to drop. In order to do this you start sideways on to the line of flight. The weight is on the left foot and the left knee is bent. Take the muzzles as far back as the cage will allow. As the targets appear the muzzles lock on to the leading bird and as they accelerate through it the gun is fired. Without pausing the upper body makes a quarter turn, the weight shifts almost entirely on to the left foot, the left knee straightens, and as the muzzles accelerate to the second target, the shot is fired, apparently directly at it. Using this technique both targets are shot extremely rapidly, before they have had much chance to drop. Personally, I find this method more effective, as I prefer to attack targets but I must emphasize that it requires exemplary gun control, and places great emphasis on your gun-mounting skills. It is not suited to the faint-hearted, as once you call for the bird you are committed and any hesitation is fatal. Once mastered, though, it can prove very effective, particularly if you shoot with an aggressive style and really like to attack your targets.

CROSSING TARGETS

Crossing targets of varying angles and speeds will be found at all Sporting shoots. Many beginners who quickly master the oncoming and going away targets, encounter serious difficulty when confronted with crossers. I am sure that much of this difficulty stems from a preoccupation with forward allowance, or lead. The beginner is too concerned with the precise feet and inches, and gives scant attention to technique and stance. If your preparation is unsound, your shooting becomes uncoordinated. Likewise, any attempt to measure deliberate lead destroys natural rhythm, and usually leads to the swing stopping at the moment of firing. As with all types of target, successful shooting at crossers depends on correct preparation prior to calling for the bird.

Position the feet so that you are facing the point where you expect to break the target, thus ensuring that the moment of firing occurs in that part of your swing where you have maximum freedom of body movement. This is essential; if your stance causes you to fire as your swing becomes restricted, the gun will be

The ready position for pairs from behind. The alternative way: the first target is shot as an overhead crossover and the body turns to take the second target as a high going away. Good gun-mounting is vital using this method.

62

slowing down as you engage the target, and it is unlikely that any amount of lead will save you from a miss.

So, stand facing the 'breaking point'. Turn the body back towards the trap, so that the muzzles are held on the flightline of the target(s), about half-way between the trap and the 'breaking point'. Do not point the muzzles at the trap, as the emerging target will have travelled some distance before your eyes and brain register it and body reacts to it. This will leave you scrabbling across the sky trying to catch the target up, with the inevitable result that you will miss behind — not through lack of forward allowance, but because your body never had a chance of responding correctly.

By holding the gun some way out from the trap you give the brain time to register the emergence of the clay(s) and as the target reaches your 'pick up' point the eyes and muzzles lock on to it and accelerate with it. As this happens the stock is sliding into the shoulder as the muzzles track the target. When the stock is in position the muzzles accelerate through the target and the shot is taken. The important thing here is that the gun is moved faster than the target. This cuts down on the amount of perceived lead that is required to break the clay.

Apparent lead, or forward allowance, will vary from person to person — what seems like ten inches to one shooter might be interpreted as two

gate lengths by another—so you must practise crossers until you have built up a sight picture for yourself as to required leads. In practising this you are in effect programming that wonderful human computer, the brain. The bigger the shooting programme in your brain, the greater your ability to cope with a wide variety of differing targets. Experience is built up by continual practice, and it is the experienced shooter who is generally the winner. So, develop your own set of lead pictures but only after perfecting your gun-mounting and target address technique.

Crossing Pairs

When a pair of crossing targets are released simultaneously, the maxim is to shoot the rear one first. This enables you to accelerate the gun along the flightpath to, and through, the second target.

BOLTING RABBITS

Another 'classic' Sporting stand, the Bolting Rabbit is great fun to shoot but can prove extremely frustrating. The target is usually presented as a crosser but there are a number of essential differences that distinguish it from conventional airborne targets.

The Bolting Rabbit clay has a

Shooting a high incomer. Care must be taken to maintain the swing without dropping the right shoulder.

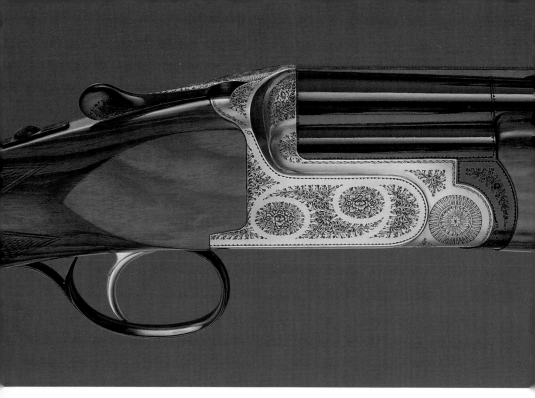

A deluxe Grade Perazzi.

British and English Open Champion 1989, George Digweed.

Brian Hebditch from Gunmark competing at the World Championships.

The Ever colourful Tina Merrick.

Waiting for the Bolting Bunny.

The author at the South of Scotland Shooting School.

The first professional Clay Shoot to be held in the UK.

Michel Carrega, four times world champion, shooting at Bois De Boulogne.

La Port 185 Automatic Trap.

George Digweed, collecting his trophy at the 1989 British Open.

Dynamo Rangers, Moscow USSR.

Former World Sporting Champion,
Barry Simpson.

Paul Bentley in action.

World Ladies Champion, Denise Eure, competing in the British Open, 1989.

DTL squad in action; the shorts are not compulsory.

Former Commonwealth Champion, Peter Boden, in action on Moscow's Dynamo Range.

The clubhouse at Bois De Boulogne, one of the oldest shooting ranges in France.

stronger rim construction than conventional clays to enable it to travel along the ground without breaking, leading to increased weight. This feature, combined with the fact that the clay makes contact with the ground, reduces the speed of the target. However, because the clay runs against a solid background, it gives the impression that it is travelling extremely fast. This is a prime example of where the presentation of a target can fool the eye, and in fooling the eye confuse the brain.

When assuming the stance to shoot these targets, it is important to remember that you are generally shooting down on the target. So often I see shooters addressing a rabbit trap with their gun muzzles held feet above the line of the target. This means that when the rabbit appears the muzzles must be pulled down as the gun is mounted. This wastes time, destroys smoothness, and distracts the eyes from the target. It is essential to hold the muzzles on the rabbit's running line. Sometimes this will require a decided lean forward on to the front foot. Hold the muzzles a few feet out from where the clay appears and be prepared to respond to its appearance instantly. As the target emerges, the muzzles accelerate with it as the stock slides into the shoulder. As the stock makes contact, the trigger is pulled with the gun still accelerating. Unless it is a very long shot, this should give the impression of shooting directly at the target with no apparent

lead. The secret of success is the acceleration of the gun as you mount into the target. Mastering this target is all about timing.

There are a few points to watch when shooting 'Bolting Bunnies'. Because of their deceiving speed it is easy to shoot in front of them. This is not always apparent, as the shot kicking up the ground can easily fool the shooter into thinking he has missed behind. What happens is that by the time the shooter's eyes register the shot striking the earth, the rabbit clay has travelled on, giving the impression that the shot was behind the target. This can easily be the cause of shooters trying to overlead rabbits.

Another problem with Bolting Rabbits is their inconsistency. Some of them bear more than a passing resemblance to kangeroos as they bounce across the ground. This is where the more instinctive method of shooting enables you to respond to these variations. An interesting point here is that the new automatic rabbit traps, such as the LaPorte, give far more consistent targets than manual traps. This is because the initial launch of the target is directly along the ground, whereas the manual trap tends to throw slightly down into the ground. The other main problem with these targets is the number of broken targets that will emerge. These 'no birds' (or, more correctly, rabbits) can be very frustrating, and if encountered, you must guard against increasing tension making your shooting become erratic. Stay calm, and be fully prepared for a regulation target every time you call 'pull'. It is so easy after a succession of 'no birds' to be caught unawares when a proper target finally emerges. Again automatic rabbit traps seem to give noticeably less broken targets than the manual types. It is worth noting that if you encounter this problem of broken targets during a major shoot, it may well be worth asking for the 'run' to be cleared of pieces of broken target before you shoot. A run littered with broken bits is going to increase the problem of targets breaking before you can shoot them.

THE TOWER

The term 'tower' covers any structure or feature of the landscape which is utilized to present higher targets. On the majority of shooting grounds these are not particularly high and present few additional problems whatever the style of target thrown. The targets from a low to medium tower are well within range of open bored guns and Skeet cartridges, and the shooting technique is much the same as that employed against targets thrown from ground level traps. However there is the genuine high tower, like the famous one at the West London Shooting Ground. Such towers are usually the feature that distinguishes top flight competitions from the rest. Very few shooting grounds have genuine high towers.

The high tower is very unforgiving and any failings in your shooting technique and gun-mounting will be punished with a load of zeros on your scorecard. The big problem with this particular stand is that it tends to exaggerate any weaknesses in your stance and gun-mounting. Combine this with the difficulty in assessing why you have missed, and it's easy to see why some shooters regard shooting the high tower as something akin to a nightmare.

The first thing to consider when tackling the tower is your mental approach. You must not be defeatist. If you walk up to the stand convinced you can't hit the targets then you will miss them. You must be positive, and determined. If you are unsure you will hesitate, and on the high tower he who hesitates is most definitely lost!

Before dealing with shooting technique for the high tower, it is appropriate to discuss cartridges and chokes. I sometimes see shooters using Trap guns on tower targets in the belief that these clays are almost unbreakable. There is no need to go to such extremes even though the targets are possibly forty yards up. If you talk to instructors at any ground with a very high tower, most will regale you with stories of how youngsters with .410's regularly break these targets. Naturally, I am not advocating a .410 for difficult Sporting clays, but I think it shows that the conventional Sporting clay gun with $1/4$/$1/4$ or $1/4$/$1/2$ chokes is more than adequate for these targets. As regards

cartridges, good Sporting or Trap loads with 8 shot are ideal, indeed Skeet cartridges will break driven tower birds. The bottom line is that when you miss it is because of shooting faults rather than any inadequacies in your gun or ammunition.

Stand conventionally, with the bodyweight biassed slightly on to the front foot. Place the muzzles on the flightline of the target you intend to shoot first (established in your mind before you step into the cage), about half-way between the stand and the tower. Now look at the tower and call for the target. As the target comes to the gun your left hand and eyes lock on to it. As you swing, the gun is mounted and accelerates through the clay. It is important that the muzzles never waver off the flightline as the gun is mounted. As the muzzles accelerate positively and aggressively past the clay, the trigger is pulled and the follow through maintained. You must ensure that the swing is maintained as the gun is fired. It is very easy on these high targets to stop the gun at the instant of firing, guaranteeing a miss behind.

Laporte automatic bolting rabbit trap. This style of trap delivers the most consistent bolting rabbits with the minimum of target breakages.

PARCOURS DE CHASSE (FITASC SPORTING)

This is the Sporting game they shoot on the Continent, and it's a sport that Britain has dominated in the past two decades. Although my 'serious' discipline is Olympic Trap, I find FITASC Sporting the most enjoyable, entertaining and challenging form of shotgun shooting. I am sure this stems from the great variety of targets presented to the shooter on each stand and the lack of repetition. Unlike the free and easy format of English Sporting, FITASC Sporting is shot in squads. These are decided in a draw prior to the competition.

Normally a major competition consists of 200 targets shot over three days in 8 rounds of 25. In a round of 25 targets you will shoot on at least three different stands. On each stand the entire squad first shoots at single targets. These will be thrown from a number of traps and each target is different. By presenting different types of clay off the same trap, the shoot organizer can show many different types of shot to the competitors. After the entire squad has completed the singles, combinations of the singles are presented as doubles.

Because you go in 'cold', so to speak, the squad is shown the targets on each stand by the referee before shooting commences, and in the interests of fairness the lead shooter on each stand rotates as the round progresses. Thus number 1 in the squad shoots first on stand 1 singles, number 2 shoots first at stand 1 doubles. On stand 2, shooter number 3 opens on the singles, number 4 on the doubles and so on.

Unfortunately this form of shooting has its drawbacks — notably that of cost, due to the increased number of trappers required in presenting such a variety of targets on each layout. Also there is a finite number of entries that a ground can handle for any particular shoot. Nowadays, nearly every event is oversubscribed and the sport is booming. Because of this the international governing body (FITASC) have been experimenting with changes to the rules to produce a format that will keep down the costs and allow more entries. On the face of it this seems a commendable move, but in altering the rules they are changing the game to a 'bastardized' form of English Sporting.

Most of the FITASC Sporting shooters in this country are opposed to any change, and I, for one, hope they are successful in resisting these alterations. If the governing body gets its way, it will have destroyed the charm, and integrity, of what is probably the finest form of competitive clayshooting.

A WORD ON TARGETS

As Sporting, in both its forms, has become so popular, an element of 'beat the shooter' has crept into layout design. Unfortunately, some shooting ground owners seem to get perverse pleasure out of throwing targets that are all but impossible, even to our very best shooters. The main problem with these targets is usually that they are on the extreme limits of sensible shotgun range. Some of these targets cease to be a test of a shooter's ability, more a test of his luck and the efficiency of his choke and cartridge. I think this is entirely the wrong approach to setting Sporting targets. It is perfectly possible to present challenging targets within the limits of sensible range (40 yards maximum in my opinion). All it requires is a little imagination and inventiveness. Any idiot can set up fast, almost out of range targets. It requires a little thought to make the clays challenging through subtleties of angle and presentation. Thankfully, most of our major Sporting grounds are run by people who believe targets are set in order to test the shooter, not to beat him.

TRAPSHOOTING

Worldwide there are two distinctive styles of Trapshooting. International, which encompasses Olympic, Universal and Automatic Trap; and Down-the-Line (or American Trap). The international disciplines are shot throughout the world but Down-the-Line (DTL) is confined to the Commonwealth and the Americas. International Trap is very demanding of the shooter and his equipment—inadequacies in either can be overcome at DTL, but any slight failing at International Trap is punished by missed targets.

DOWN-THE-LINE

Down-the-Line (or DTL) is the oldest, and most basic, of all the Trap disciplines. It was the first of the formal clayshooting disciplines and

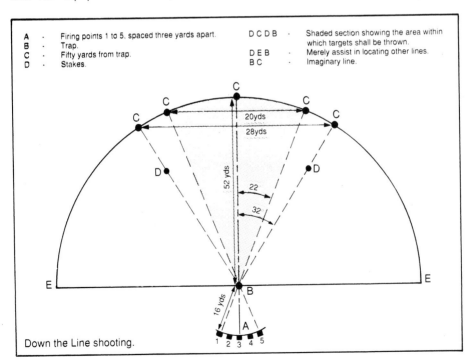

A	-	Firing points 1 to 5, spaced three yards apart.
B	-	Trap.
C	-	Fifty yards from trap.
D	-	Stakes.

D C D B	-	Shaded section showing the area within which targets shall be thrown.
D E B	-	Merely assist in locating other lines.
B C	-	Imaginary line.

Down the Line shooting.

developed out of live pigeon shooting. The original form utilized five traps set in a straight line in front of the shooter. This was modified in the 1880s by W.G. Sargent from Missouri. His system of shooting used three traps set about four feet apart, which threw targets at random angles. At the turn of the century, the 'Sargent' system was superseded by a single 'auto-angling' trap. which changed the angles at random as the trap was cocked. Interestingly, when I first started shooting clays, CPSA literature on DTL still referred to the 'Sargent' system as a means of holding informal DTL shoots.

The main development in recent years in DTL has been the introduction of electric traps. These are used for virtually all DTL competitions — only the smallest clubs still retain the manually cocked trap. The most famous of the electric traps is, without doubt, the Winchester White Flyer. It throws superb regulation DTL targets and is easily the most popular DTL trap in use today. There are other electric DTL traps available, including some manufactured in Britain. Notable amongst the British traps are the Sidewinder and the Farey.

Recently, there have been attempts to introduce acoustic target release to DTL but this has been resisted by the shooters. Personally, I feel that opposition to acoustics is misguided. One of the big problems that DTL shooters have to contend with is inconsistent target release due to the human element. At the shooter's call, the puller has to respond by pressing the button to release the target. It's not difficult to see that during a long day the puller becomes tired and his concentration wavers. The result of this is 'slow pulls'. The adoption of acoustic release would virtually eliminate this problem and would ensure the same, consistent, target release for all the competitors.

Some years ago the CPSA experimented with acoustics at the British DTL Championships at Carlisle. Unfortunately the equipment used had not been fully tested and there were a lot of problems. This event prejudiced many DTL shooters against acoustics.

Reliable equipment is now freely available and I feel the CPSA should look again at the subject. Anything which makes the sport fairer must be a step forward.

DTL is shot over one trap machine which has a fixed elevation but constantly changing angles. The targets are thrown a distance of 55 yards, which makes them slow in comparison to the International forms of Trapshooting. The angles are also less severe than ABT or Olympic Trap. Two shots are allowed at each target, but, unlike in International Trap, the results of the first and second shots are scored differently. A hit with the first barrel scores three points, with the second barrel scores two points. The ultimate score, therefore, is 100 'kills'/300 points. A normal DTL competition is conducted over 100 targets, shot in four rounds of 25. A squad consists of five shooters, who shoot from five fixed stands 16 yards behind the traphouse. Each shooter fires in turn until the whole squad has shot at five targets. The referee will then announce 'Change' and each shooter then moves on to the next stand to shoot another five targets. This procedure follows until each shooter has shot five targets on each stand, making 25 in all.

DTL is certainly the 'tamest' of the Trap disciplines in terms of target speed and angles. Because of this some shooters are rather scornful of it. This scorn is certainly based on ignorance. Whilst a single DTL target may be technically easy to shoot, stringing together 100 first barrel 'kills' is no easy matter, and to win the British DTL Championship is every bit as hard as winning the British Grand Prix for Olympic Trap. If DTL is not your chosen discipline, don't knock it. If you think DTL is that easy, get out there and prove it—you will find it's a lot harder than you think.

DTL is a good starting point for anyone who aspires to the more difficult forms of Trapshooting. It teaches the basics of Trapshooting techniques. However, if your ambitions lie in the direction of Olympic or Universal Trap, switch to the harder discipline once you are confident you can cope with DTL. Too much DTL shooting can actually hamper your International Trapshooting. Because of the undemanding nature of DTL targets, inadequacies of style can be

overcome by intense concentration and a desire to win. When you shoot International Trap, any shortcomings in your style will result in poor scores. Therefore if you want to shoot Olympic Trap, by all means start on DTL, but progress to your intended discipline as soon as possible. If you just want to shoot DTL, you will find it a demanding and challenging sport that places more emphasis on concentration and application rather than on just pure shooting skill.

THE REGULATION TARGET

In still air the target must travel between 50 and 55 yards. The height shall be adjusted so that at a distance of 10 yards from the trap it will be a minimum of 8 feet and a maximum of 10 feet. The maximum target angles are normally 22 degrees either side of centre. The trap must be fitted with an interrupter so that it throws an unpredictable and random sequence of angles. Some of the older traps are not fitted with this device and the observant shooter could soon predict the angle of his next target. These older traps are no longer allowed for any registered competitions.

THE DOWN-THE-LINE GUN

Because DTL targets are less severe than the International Trap disciplines, many beginners think they can cope with DTL by using a multi-choke Sporting gun. This is a mistake. To shoot Trap you need a Trap gun. Because of the slower flight of DTL targets, fast handling guns can be something of a liability. I have found that a gun I can shoot well at Olympic Trap usually doesn't perform as effectively at DTL. Down-the-Line makes different demands on a gun's design. Generally a rather steadier, and heavier, gun is more suited to DTL targets. Many of the 32in barreled under-and-overs are particularly suited to this discipline. It is very easy to overshoot on DTL targets, so a little extra weight helps smooth out the swing and reduce any tendency to jump the target.

Most Trap guns are stocked to shoot slightly high in relation to the point of aim. Whilst this is a disadvantage on a gun for International Trap, it can be a positive advantage on a DTL gun. This is because DTL targets are thrown at a constant elevation, with no daisy-cutters or skyscrapers. The slightly higher stock enables the shooter to 'float' the clay on the end of the barrel at the moment of pulling the trigger, confident in the knowledge that his shot pattern will cover the bird. I also feel that a slightly longer stock is also beneficial for DTL. An extra ½in on the length will help check any overswinging or erratic gun movements. To be really successful at DTL, you must concentrate on being extremely smooth and consistent in your gun movement. Select a gun that helps you attain this. There is no

place in DTL for the rather explosive technique that proves effective on some of the faster Trap disciplines.

THE DOWN-THE-LINE CARTRIDGE

Until 1 January 1990, under CPSA rules the maximum permitted shot load for DTL was 32g with a maximum shot size of No. 6 (English). In view of the reduction in the shot load imposed by the International Shooting Union on disciplines under their control, the four home associations reduced the maximum permitted shot load to 28g. This does not pose any problems for DTL shooters. 28g cartridges are more than adequate for DTL. Indeed, experience with the lighter load at Olympic Trap indicates that there is little difference in the winning scores. The only problem that could occur is a psychological one. If you believe that you are being handicapped by 28g loads then you will be. So, when the reduction comes into force, put any doubts out of your mind and get on with the shooting! If you have been used to the heavier shot load but approach 28g cartridges with an open mind, you might be surprised at how effective they are.

There are many top quality cartridges on the market, yet I never cease to be amazed by the number of shooters who select their cartridge purely on the grounds of cost. When you consider the overall expense of shooting a major competition, trying to save on cartridges seems false economy. Try a number of different brands and select a shell that suits your timing and your gun. Buy the very best that you can afford. It might only make one target difference in a thousand, but that one target may be the one that wins you the British DTL Championship.

CHOKE

The majority of Trap guns come out of the factory with between ¾ and full choke in the bottom barrel. With modern cartridges this is too much for DTL. Many top Olympic Trap shooters use ½ choke for the first barrel and there is no need for anything tighter at DTL. A good 'kill' is one where the target is 'blown to bits' rather than smoked. A splodge of black dust hanging in the air looks very impressive but signifies a pattern so tight that there can be little margin for error. The rules only require you to break a visible piece from the target and there are no extra points for annihilating it. Naturally a pattern that only broke targets into two pieces would not inspire confidence, but there is no need to go to the other extreme. ½ choke should produce good breaks on targets caught in the centre of the pattern and at the same time the wider spread may pick up an extra target or two that you would have missed with a full choke. Unless you are an unbelievably fast shot, the top barrel should be bored full choke.

DOWN-THE-LINE TECHNIQUE

A look at the top shooters at any major DTL tournament would reveal a number of different styles and techniques, including some weird and wonderful ones. It is possible to shoot excellent scores at DTL with some rather dubious styles, the concentration and determination of the shooter overcoming any deficiencies in shooting technique. For this reason, DTL can prove a poor training ground for the international forms of Trapshooting. It is vitally important that you start with a sound basic technique. This will not only enable you to progress to the faster Trap disciplines, but will also help you cope with those days when the DTL targets are flying erratically, assisted by our wonderful British weather.

As in all forms of shooting, good preparation before calling for the target is essential. Although the slower speed of DTL targets allow a little more time to deliver the shot, once you have called for the target you are committed, and should move positively and confidently. It is bad practice to be rectifying preparation faults as your eyes and the gun are attempting to lock on to the target.

The essentials for good DTL shooting are simple. See the target quickly, and break it quickly. Shooters often ask when should they be breaking the

target. The answer is as soon as they comfortably, and competently, are able. The longer you take to fire, the further away the target becomes, and the chances for error increase with every split second you waste. Additionally, slow shooting tends to introduce an element of deliberate aiming. This is a marvellous technique for rifle shooting but you never aim with a shotgun. Attempting to take deliberate aim almost invariably leads to the gun stopping as the trigger is pulled and consequently an inevitable miss. It is very tempting, because of the slower speed of DTL targets, to ride out the target, and attempt to 'make sure' of it. Never do this. The more deliberate your shooting becomes, the less your natural hand/eye co-ordination comes into play, and an element of aiming creeps in without you realizing it. If this happens it is very hard to keep your timing, and good timing is the key to all forms of Trapshooting.

STANCE AND FOOTWORK

A correct stance is the cornerstone around which success at Trapshooting is built. Some good DTL shooters manage to return impressive scores with less than perfect stances, but I am convinced that any fault in basic technique will one day let you down when the pressure is on, and to be successful at any competitive sport you must be able to perform under pressure.

Poor trapshooting style. The body is twisted and the right heel is situated to the left of the front foot. This gives poor balance.

The basic stance is the same for all forms of Trapshooting. It is essential to have complete freedom of movement of the body in any plane in which the gun has to be moved. It must be possible to swing freely to left and right without any tightening of the body. If this is neglected, you will find that you will run out of body movement and will be forcing the gun to move against the pull of those muscles that are under strain. This will inevitably lead to a checking of the swing and this will cause the occasional miss, something you can't afford at a discipline as competitive as DTL.

Therefore stand naturally with the feet 8 to 10 inches apart. I feel that an upright stance is best, although some shooters favour a slight bend of the left knee. This is permissible, but guard against any exaggeration creeping in. If the knee is bent too much, it pushes the weight of the body too far over the left foot and puts part of your muscle structure under pressure. This makes good balance and sharp response impossible.

If a line from the centre of the stand to the trap is taken as twelve o'clock, the feet should be positioned so that the toes of the left foot are pointing to one o'clock and the right foot points to three o'clock. A line drawn through the ankle of the right foot and the big toe of the left foot should point to twelve o'clock, directly at the centre of the traphouse. When the gun is mounted it should lie over, and along, this line between the right

Good solid stance. Feet are positioned naturally with the body weight slightly biassed on the front foot. The body can respond rapidly in any direction. A target can be found without any loss of balance or gun control.

77

ankle and the left toe. The weight should be positioned slightly over the front foot, distributed 60 per cent over the left foot, 40 per cent on the right foot. Guard against pushing the body weight too far forward as this jeopardizes balance and inhibits smooth movement of the body.

You will no doubt see DTL shooters who stand much squarer to the traphouse than I have recommended. This can create problems on the extreme right-hand targets as it causes the shooter to use arm movement to maintain gun swing. This in turn can cause the cheek to lose contact with the stock, resulting in the gun no longer shooting where you are looking. The square on stance is totally unsuitable for the International Trap disciplines so I suggest you follow the above style.

GUN-MOUNTING

It is preferable that the gun and body move towards the target as one integrated unit. The gun should be positioned comfortably in the shoulder pocket — *not* out on the top of the arm. This is most important. The top of the stock should be almost level with the top of the shoulder, enabling you to place your head on the stock without any undue bending of the neck. The gun should be placed firmly against the shoulder but on no account should it be pulled back into position. Pulling back causes the shoulder to move back as well, and

places the muscles in the shoulder, neck, and upper back under strain. This has an adverse effect on body movement and also reduces the shoulder's ability to absorb recoil. Always position the gun to the face and to the shoulder in exactly the same place every time. Consistency is vital, particularly at DTL, where there is no margin for error. One second barrel can put you out of the running, so ensure that your gun-mounting is perfect. Practise it until it becomes second nature.

Hold the forend at a position that feels comfortable and allows you to control your swing. Guard against holding the forend too close to the action as this can give too much leverage to the left hand, resulting in an erratic swing. Personally, when shooting DTL, I tend to place the left hand further forward on the forend than I would when shooting Olympic Trap. I find this slows up my timing to match the less severe targets.

PREPARATION

Having worked out how to stand and mount the gun, the next problem is where to point and where to look. There are two schools of thought on this in DTL. The first, and conventional, style is to hold on the roof of the traphouse. The alternative is to hold the muzzles above the traphouse, partway along the vertical flight of the clay. I would recommend beginners to start by holding on the traphouse roof as this enables them to see the target almost at the moment it appears. This gives a more natural swing and timing which can be modified in the light of experience; but don't experiment with a high gun position till you are reasonably competent at the conventional style.

At this point the shooter's hold position is only half decided. Because the possible extreme target angles are different on each of the five stands, it is a decided advantage to vary the lateral hold of the muzzles as you progress from station to station. The general rule is that you hold on the left corner of the traphouse on station 1, the right corner on station 5, and dead centre on station 3. Station 2 hold is half-way between the left corner and the centre, Station 4 half-way between the right corner and the centre. Again, these positions can be modified with experience, and a little experimentation in practice will establish the best placings for your timing.

With the hold position decided, you must determine where to look for the target prior to calling. There are two golden rules here:

1. Do not look at the traphouse.

2. Do not look at the foresight.

These rules are absolute! If you break either of them you will find that the target will have moved some way along its flightpath before your eyes switch focus to it. This will destroy your natural timing, with disastrous consequences. It is worth noting here that even a second barrel at DTL can be a disaster to an AA class shooter.

The correct way is to mount your gun, taking the hold position for that particular stand, and before you call for the target, shift your vision out beyond the traphouse, and really look hard for the clay. Your whole concentration must now be directed towards seeing that target as soon as it appears.

MAKING THE SHOT

You are now at the stage where your hold position is determined, your gun is mounted, and your eyes and all your concentration are focused on seeing the target. In short, you are ready to call 'pull'.

At whatever discipline of Trap you decide to shoot, always cultivate a sharp, clear call. Indistinct grunts and groans often result in a slow pull, the puller being unsure of your call. Make the guy on the button jump—you'll get much better pulls! Calling clearly is a good habit to get into if you intend to progress to the international forms of Trap as these are generally shot via an acoustic release. Bad calls often fail to activate acoustics and a series of 'no birds' is very damaging to your concentration.

You are ready to shoot. A clear call, your eyes lock on to the target and your gun and body move together, accelerating smoothly after the clay.

As the muzzles accelerate through the target, the trigger is pulled and the clay breaks. Everything should be smooth and instinctive. If your preparation is perfect, making the shot will be simple as you have done the bulk of the work before calling 'pull'. There is no time for corrections once the target is on its way. Be 101 per cent prepared before calling and your shot will be delivered instinctively and successfully.

COMPETITION

Most DTL shooters have a preference as to who they will shoot with in a squad. I feel it is a good idea for the beginner to ignore this. When competing, you should be oblivious to the other squad members. So long as you do nothing to distract them, you should shoot your own timing and style. Do not allow yourself to be rushed along by a quick squad. You are not shooting as part of a team, you are an individual, so don't be distracted by the others on the line. I feel it is a mistake always to shoot in the same squad. If you can shoot with anyone alongside you, you will find it much easier to face the pressure of a shoot-off, if the occasion should arise. For the same reason, it is a mistake always to start on the same station in every match. I realize that this advice is flying in the face of DTL convention, but I feel that the more flexible a shooter is, the more easily he can adapt to different conditions and circumstances. This makes for a much tougher competitor.

CONCENTRATION

Obviously in a discipline as demanding as DTL, absolute concentration is paramount. DTL is unique in Trap-shooting, in that it is the only discipline where five shots are taken successively on a stand before moving to the next. It is vital that you guard against letting your concentration wander after you have shot a couple of targets. You must maintain your concentration throughout all five targets. By all means relax as you move to the next stand, but when the referee calls 'ready', focus your concentration on the job in hand.

VARIATIONS ON THE DOWN-THE-LINE THEME

Single Barrel

The Commonwealth countries are peculiar in that they allow two shots at DTL targets. In America, all DTL, or American Trapshooting (ATA), is shot single barrel. In Britain there are a limited number of single barrel competitions held each year. I feel that this a great shame as single barrel DTL is more challenging shooting than the regular two barrel version. It is also cheaper for the beginner, as only 100 cartridges are required. Similarly, quality single barrel Trap guns are considerably cheaper than under-and-overs. I think a switch to single barrel shooting at DTL could increase the popularity of the sport, but, unfortunately, any move in this direction, is likely to meet strong opposition from the traditionalists.

Double Rise

As its name suggests, this is DTL with two targets instead of one! Again this is not that popular in Britain. I feel that its lack of appeal is due to the poor quality of doubles thrown in this country. If shooting grounds would throw good regulation doubles I think they would get more entries. Sadly, as Double Rise is such a subordinate discipline to DTL, that the attitude seems to be 'anything goes'. I think the CPSA should adopt the American ATA rules and try to promote Double Rise shooting instead of treating it as an afterthought.

Handicap

Another rarely seen variation of DTL; the handicapping is done by distance. The better you shoot, the further back from the trap you stand. In Britain, the maximum handicap distance is 23 yards but the Americans make it much more challenging. Their 'back line' is at 27 yards, and it is considered a great achievement to shoot well enough to make the 27 yard line.

Reading the above, I seem to be advocating all things American for

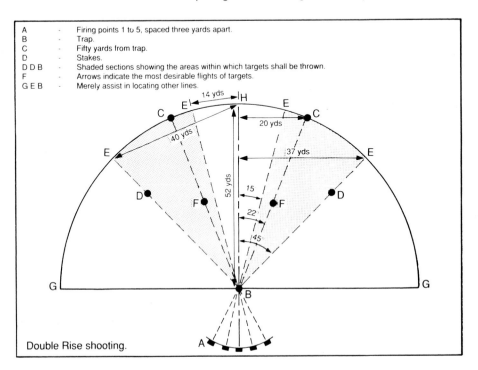

A	-	Firing points 1 to 5, spaced three yards apart.
B	-	Trap.
C	-	Fifty yards from trap.
D	-	Stakes.
D D B	-	Shaded sections showing the areas within which targets shall be thrown.
F	-	Arrows indicate the most desirable flights of targets.
G E B	-	Merely assist in locating other lines.

Double Rise shooting.

81

DTL shooting. On reflection this doesn't seem a bad thing. The ATA rules make DTL a more interesting and challenging game, and I think their adoption would increase the popularity of DTL over here.

INTERNATIONAL TRAP

First, the gun. Most Trap guns are made with high stocks and shoot above the point of aim, and although most of the pundits recommend a high stocked/high shooting gun for the Trap disciplines, it is an interesting fact that the majority of the world's top Olympic Trap shooters use relatively flat shooting guns. The US Army Marksmanship Unit at Fort Benning also strongly recommend that the Olympic Trap gun be stocked in a way that, when correctly mounted, the eyes look straight down the rib, and the gun shoots to point of aim.

My own experience is that this is entirely correct for Olympic Trap. The reasons for this are the great variation between the lowest and highest targets on an International Trap range, and the fact that the lower targets will have begun to drop slightly before a second barrel can be fired at them. In these circumstances it is very easy, with a high shooting gun, to miss over the top of the target. International Trap is very much a reaction sport and once that target is on its way there is no time to make allowances for high shooting.

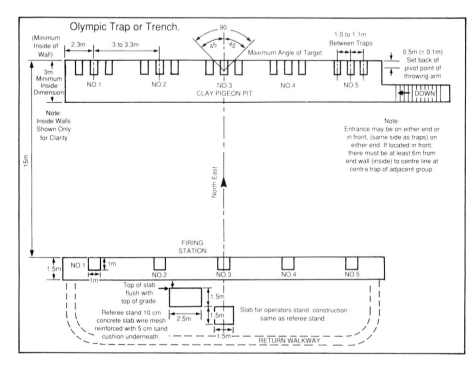

If the gun shoots where you look, all you have to do is look at the target and pull the trigger. Simple! The gun fit, therefore, should be such that the eye is looking straight down the rib, with a stock length suitable for the individual. Any more than a very slight degree of cast is to be avoided if at all possible. Trap guns with excessive cast kick like mules and are most uncomfortable to shoot. This does not make for good scores. A good coach can usually avoid the need for cast by working on the shooter's technique and stance.

The International Trap gun is almost invariably an under-and-over. The ideal would vary from shooter to shooter, but a basic specification would be 30-32in barrels, bottom barrel choked between ½ and ¾ choke, top barrel full choke. The overall weight should be between 7½ and 8½lbs depending on the shooter's physique. The gun should balance just forward of the hinge pin, having a slight bias towards the muzzle. This slight muzzle-heaviness can be increased by the use of 32in barrels. It reduces muzzle flip and makes the gun much steadier on the second shot which is all-important at International Trap where the second shot scores the same as the first. The trigger pulls should be crisp and between 3-4lbs in weight. If they are much heavier than this, get them adjusted. The foregoing specification applies equally to Universal and Automatic Trap with, perhaps, a slightly more open choke on the first barrel for Universal Trap where the targets are slightly slower.

A word of caution: when using a gun with a very light trigger-pull, **DO NOT SLAM** the gun closed. In fact, whatever the weight of the trigger-pulls, never slam a gun closed. Violently closing a gun dramatically increases mechanical wear and adds to the chance of the gun firing accidentally.

TECHNIQUE

The fastest targets thrown in Trapshooting are from an Olympic Trap range. In addition the angles are fierce. You only have split seconds to find and shoot the target. It follows that your preparation must be complete and your concentration at maximum *before* the target is called. Once the shooter has called 'Pull' he is committed and must move instantly and positively. Any errors in reacting to the target are usually caused by mistakes made before the target is called for. I strongly believe that the result of any particular shot is 80 per cent decided before you call for it. Because of the requirement for instantaneous reaction the preparation *before* the call must be perfect otherwise hitting the clay becomes chance, hardly an ideal basis for a good result. Concentration is paramount. Focus your mind. Don't let the performance of your fellow squad members distract you. It is too late to alter a bad gun mount or sharpen

your mind after the target is on its way; the chances are, two barrels later, it is away for good.

STANCE AND FOOTWORK

It is important to stand in a manner which allows full freedom of movement of the body from the ankles upwards. This means standing in a normal manner with no exaggerated crouches or contortions. Stand upright with the feet evenly balanced. When mounting the gun, the balance is shifted slightly on to the front foot. To ensure an uninterrupted swing to left and right, good positioning of the feet is essential. Experience has shown me that the best foot position is as follows:

If dead ahead is taken as twelve o'clock, then the left foot should be positioned pointing to one o'clock and the right foot pointing to three o'clock. The feet should be spaced no more than 8–10 inches apart. A line drawn through the heel of the right foot and the toe of the left foot should point to twelve o'clock; when mounted in the shoulder the gun should be positioned exactly over this line between right heel and left toe. (Left-handers should reverse all these instructions.)

Correct position from the right-hand side. Note how the shoulder pushes into the gun. It is not pulled back.

GUN-MOUNTING

Obviously this is a most critical part of preparation as it governs where the gun points in relation to the line of sight. Also, bad gun-mounting increases the effect of recoil. The gun should be placed in a comfortable position in the shoulder, with the top of the comb almost level with the top of the shoulder. This should allow the face to meet the stock without any undue strain on the muscles in the neck or shoulder. The gun should not be pulled back into the shoulder, as this tends to tighten the muscles and adversely affects the way the body can move. It also removes much of the natural elasticity of the shoulder which results in more recoil being transmitted to the body's skeleton. This can result in back and neck problems in a prolonged shooting career. Some shooters (myself included) tend to push the face forward along the comb of the stock; this creates tension in the upper back and is best avoided. Unfortunately, when a shooter has been doing it for years it is a hard habit to break!

Mount the gun in a way that feels comfortable to you. Some shooters like to point the gun high as they mount and then bring the muzzles down to the traphouse; others prefer to bring the gun to the shoulder with barrels pointing at the mark. Both are effective, so the individual should experiment to see which system gives the best results. It is essential to position the gun to the face and shoulder in exactly the same place every time. The gun and body must move as one unit, with the movement of the body being directed to the gun through face and shoulder contact, and the grip of the right hand. The left hand is only to support the gun and make the gun and body a complete unit, rather like a tank turret. The left hand must not be used to point the gun at the target before the rest of the body moves. Everything must move together.

The position of the left hand on the forend will affect the speed and control of gun movement. If the hand is placed well forward on the forend, it will make the swing slower and smoother, but it will restrict the amount of horizontal movement available to the shooter. Conversely, if the forend is held right back at the action, the swing becomes much faster but control of the gun becomes erratic. Obviously the ideal lies somewhere between the two. You must experiment to find the best position, taking into account such factors as barrel weight and point of balance. The grip on the forend must be firm enough to control the barrels under recoil but guard against creating unnecessary tension in the upper arms.

PREPARATION

Once the gun is in the shoulder, the next problem is where to point it and where to look for the target. There can be no hard and fast rules on this as it will vary from layout to layout depending on background, target visibility and light conditions. If the clays are hard to see it often pays to hold the gun below the aiming mark; if the wind is affecting them it often helps to hold the gun above the mark. There is no definitive rule on this, and it will vary from shooter to shooter. Everyone should experiment in practice to find the optimum hold under a wide variety of conditions. The big mistake is always to hold in the same place come hell or high water. It may work most of the time but every now and then such a rigid technique will be unable to cope with the prevailing conditions. The more adaptable and experienced a competitor is, the better chance he has of mastering the great variations in weather and light conditions found in this country.

When you have decided where to point the muzzles, the next thing to consider is where to look for the target. This is very easy to decide. Stand behind the layout where you will be shooting next and watch the clays. Unless you have bionic eyes you won't be able to see them the instant they appear. For the first couple of yards they seem blurred, and then after about five yards they will be recognizable as a distinct target. This is the area you should be looking in, not at the mark on the

Correct position from the left-hand side. Note the forend grip.

traphouse roof. Do not look at a fixed point but expand your vision to cover an area as wide and as deep as possible out in front of the trench. Anything that moves in this area catches the eye and as it comes into sharp focus as a target, the gun moves towards it. It is important that no movement is made before the target is properly identified. Moving after a blurred target will mean that you do not have an exact line on it and you will be searching to establish that line when you should be pulling the trigger. Likewise, if you focus intently on the traphouse mark, the target will have travelled a greater distance before the eyes can react to it. The result of this will either be that you never catch up with the clay, or a panic stricken jump of the gun in an attempt to intercept it.

MAKING THE SHOT

See it, shoot it. Sounds too simple, but this is the basis of good Trapshooting. Prepare for the shot correctly, look in the right place, be alert, and you have already done eighty per cent of the work. Now all you have to do is see the target, move the gun to it, and pull the trigger. There is no time at OT to think of forward allowance or maintained lead. See the target clearly, accelerate the gun along the flightline, and as you reach the clay the trigger is pulled with the gun still accelerating. The eyes are focused firmly on the target at all times. If the gun is mounted properly and you are standing correctly, the eyes will pick up the target, the gun will follow the eyes and your natural timing and reactions will deliver the shot successfully. Good preparation enables your instinctive reactions to operate. Once the target is on its way there is no time to think, just to react.

THE SECOND BARREL

In many ways International Trap is a second barrel game. I am always amazed to see shooters pulling faces when they score with the second shot. The time to grimace is when both barrels have missed. It is very rare for a high score to be shot at International Trap without the use of the second barrel. A shooter is only as good as the effectiveness of his second shot. Although highly improbable, it is theoretically possible to miss all the targets with the first barrel and still win the shoot. I have seen J.R. (Bob) Braithwaite shoot 25 straight of which 18 were second barrel kills. Bob went on to win the shoot. Thus an effective second barrel can be the difference between disaster and success.

To be really good with the second barrel requires much practice. The 'chuck and chance it' technique is not

Top Italian trap shooter Albano Pera, just prior to shooting. A study in concentration!

88

consistent. The shooter must get back on to the line of the clay instantly, and then accelerate through it, pulling the trigger for the second time. Because of the speed of the target, there is no time for a deliberate and conscious correction to be made. The shooter's eyes and gun must seek the target out again and instinctively deliver the shot. Any hesitation is fatal. In order to keep the second barrel response effective, it is a good idea to occasionally shoot at the pieces of targets broken with the first barrel. This keeps the second barrel ticking over nicely until it's needed in anger. Finally, don't be concerned if you are hitting a lot of second barrels — at least they are on the scoreboard! You shouldn't be concentrating on breaking all the targets with the first barrel, just concern yourself with breaking ALL the targets. There are no extra points for style and 25 second barrels beats 24 first barrels and 1 miss.

UNIVERSAL TRAP

The same shooting technique applies to all the International Trapshooting disciplines but there are one or two points worth noting for Universal Trap and ABT. At Universal you will be covering one group of five traps from all the shooting stands. It can be advantageous to alter where you point the gun from station to station. At Peg 1 hold it about two feet to the left of the mark; at Peg 2 hold

one foot to the left; at Peg 3 hold on the mark; at Peg 4 hold one foot to the right; and at Peg 5 hold two feet to the right.

Universal Trap targets are not quite as fast as those in Olympic Trap but the extreme angles are more acute. Therefore it is very important to adopt a stance which allows complete freedom of movement whilst still retaining complete control of the swing.

AUTOMATIC TRAP (ABT)

Again the same basic technique applies, but there is a difference between ABT and the two senior International disciplines. ABT uses one multi-oscillating trap. Because of the way a single trap is installed, the angle targets will not cross in front of the mark. The right-hand targets will

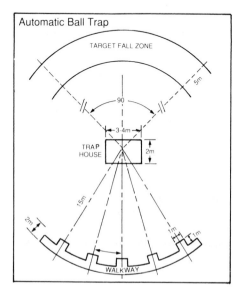

Automatic Ball Trap

appear to the right of the aiming point, the left hand targets to the left. To prevent yourself being taken unawares by this it pays to hold the muzzles somewhat lower than at Universal or Olympic. This enables you to pick up the line of flight over the muzzles of the gun, avoiding having to move the barrels laterally to cover a target that seems to have appeared six feet to the right or left of where you are looking.

International Trap in its three forms is a challenging game. In motor racing terms it would equate to Formulas One (Olympic Trap), Two (Universal) and Three (ABT). In its Olympic and Universal forms, it is an international sport at the very highest level. ABT provides enjoyable competition and is a good stepping stone between Down-the-Line and Olympic Trap. Indeed, if suitable traps are used and correctly installed, ABT provides good practice for the Olympic discipline at considerably less cost.

The important word here is suitable. Unfortunately, due to the considerable latitude allowed by the ISU rules, some grounds throw very tame ABT targets, barely more than 'souped up' DTL with variable elevation. If you intend to use ABT to practise for Olympic Trap, choose a ground that has European machines that are correctly adjusted to throw the maximum targets. Practice on tame ABT targets will leave you inadequately prepared for Olympic Trap.

UIT DOUBLE TRAP

For a number of years the Executive Committee of the UIT have been endeavouring to develop a completely new shotgun event for international competition. In the early 1970s there was some suggestion that some form of double-rise shooting would be introduced to supplement, or, possibly even replace, Olympic Trap. Although proposals were put forward, the idea was soon shelved in the face of opposition from most of the European shooting federations. The situation remained thus, until the 1984 Olympics. At the Los Angeles Games, the shooting sports came under a great deal of pressure and at one stage it seemed as if there would be no shooting included in the Olympic programme. This was due partly to the strong anti-gun lobby in California, and partly to the supposed lack of spectator appeal of shooting.

As the Olympics have become increasingly commercialized, the American television companies have had more of a say in how the Games should be run, and what sports should be included. This commercial pressure has resulted in the introduction of 'professional' sports such as tennis, into the Olympic programme. At the same time, the International Olympic Committee has been forced by the power of money to take a long, hard, look at the television appeal of the minor sports. This has resulted in the IOC directing the UIT to improve the format of the shooting sports in order to make them more televizable. Implicit in this directive was the veiled threat that if the UIT failed to make shooting more exciting in television terms, there was a strong possibility the sport would be excluded from the Olympic programme. At the same time, the IOC implied that it would look favourably on additional shooting disciplines developed specifically to appeal on television.

Faced with this, the UIT altered the format of the established Olympic shooting disciplines to include a final that could provide a televizable climax to any shooting event. Additionally, they decided to develop a new form of clay target shooting that would meet the criteria laid down by the IOC. To assist them in this, the UIT approached Conny Wirnhier to develop the new discipline on their behalf. Conny was one of the world's leading Skeet shooters in the 1960s and 1970s, winning the Gold medal in the 1972 Olympics. Since his retirement from competitive shooting he has been coaching shotgun shooting in his native West Germany.

Conny was given a number of ground rules as guidance in the development of the new discipline. These were that it should be easily televizable, easily understandable for spectators, and economical to install. The competition format should be much shorter than the three days required for the existing disciplines of Trap and Skeet, and also be more difficult, initially, to obtain maximum

scores. At the same time, the UIT, becoming conscious of the increasing environmental pressure on clay target shooting, asked Conny Wirnhier to reduce the amount of lead used in the cartridges and the level of noise generated by a competition. Taking all these factors into consideration, Conny Wirnhier set about devising the new discipline. The result of this development is UIT Double Trap.

Trapshooting, in its American and CPSA forms, has had a doubles event for many years. CPSA Double Rise involves the shooting of two DTL clays launched from the same trap. Double Trap, as its name implies, is the shooting of two simultaneously launched clay targets, but in the new game they are launched from two traps situated one metre apart in a traphouse similar to that used for Olympic or Universal Trap. The left hand trap is fixed and throws a straight target 70-72m. Now, here comes the catch. The right hand trap throws 65-67m, but is auto-angling and throws its targets between 15° to the left and 15° to the right of centre. The targets are released acoustically as in Olympic Trap. It doesn't take much imagination to realize that the fact that one target is variable makes this a very challenging form of shooting. In fact it was so challenging that noboby wanted to shoot it.

During 1989, a number of competitions for Double Trap were held in Britain and on the Continent. Entries were lukewarm to say the least, the 1989 British Grand Prix attracting 11 entries. Without exception they were won with very low scores, reflecting the difficult nature of the game. At one of the first major international competitions, held after the Grand Prix of Nations in Montecatini in 1989, British shooter Kevin Gill won with a score of 80 ex 100. This was against a field of world class shooters! A glance through the results of major competitions reveals that this is about the level of winning scores: 80 per cent. There seemed to be a marked reluctance amongst the top shooters to shoot Double Trap because they felt that the random nature of the game made it almost impossible to attain a degree of consistency at it.

It seemed that the UIT had created a discipline at which even the top shooters could not perform consistently. If the top shooters could not master it, what chance did the average shooters have? It is important to remember that the bulk of people taking part in a sport will never attain international stardom, therefore it is necessary to frame rules that will give them a reasonable level of success, whilst still retaining a challenge to the top competitors. Failure to do this can result in an elitist sport for a handful of top competitors with no grass roots from which future champions can evolve. Faced with this lack of acceptance by the shooters the UIT decided to re-think the format.

The UIT Technical Committee has been working overtime to revamp Double Trap and the first priority was to eliminate the oscillating trap. To achieve this they have replaced the two traps of the original version with three fixed traps. The discipline can now be shot on an Olympic or Universal Trap range, in addition to purpose built ranges. The three fixed traps would be numbers 7, 8 and 9 on an Olympic layout, and 2, 3 and 4 on a Universal layout.

The left hand trap is set at an angle between 0° and 15° to the *LEFT*; the centre trap is set between 5° either side of centre; and the right hand trap is set between 0° and 15° to the *RIGHT*. By setting the left hand trap to throw to the left, and the right hand trap to throw to the right, the UIT have eliminated the problem of targets crossing as they emerge.

The traps are set to throw the target to a distance between 55 and 65m at a height between 3 and 3.5m. The actual height, angle and distance settings for each individual trap is pre-determined by a set of nine schemes (similar to the system used at Olympic Trap).

One of the principal objections to the original version of Double Trap was the potential inequality of the competition due to the variable trap. The use of fixed machines goes some way to eliminating this. To make the competition totally equitable the UIT have decided that the distribution of targets will be controlled by a distributor similar to that used for Olympic Trap. This will ensure that, during a round of 25 doubles, on each of the five stands a shooter will receive 2 doubles from traps 1 and 2, two doubles from traps 2 and 3, and one double from traps 1 and 3. This will ensure that, in each round, every competitor shoots exectly the same targets. Thus Double Trap becomes a measure of skill not luck.

The competition is conducted in rounds of 25 pairs making it possible to shoot 200 targets in the same time as 100 Olympic Trap. This considerably shortens the duration of the competition, which cuts down the amount of time the local environs are subjected to the sound of gunfire. Both traps are set for elevation at the high end of the spectrum for Trap targets, the idea being to make it possible to film the competition with one fixed camera. Naturally, if there was a great variation in height between the two targets it would be impossible to show both targets being broken on the same screen.

Double Trap was the first discipline to have the maximum permitted shot load restricted to 28g, reducing the amount of lead deposited on the shooting range and at the same time bringing about a reduction in recoil and noise.

THE GUN FOR DOUBLE TRAP

A conventional Trap gun seems to be the ideal tool for this new discipline.

If you have a favourite Trap gun that you are completely familiar with then stick to it. My own feelings are that a gun which shoots exactly to point of aim is ideal. Choking should be full in the top barrel, with anything between ½ and ¾ choke in the bottom.

THE CARTRIDGE

The introduction of Double Trap heralded the introduction of the 28g shot load for international shooting. Initially, many manufacturers designated their cartridges 'Double Trap'. Since then, however, nearly all the shotgun disciplines have had their rules amended to limit the permitted shot load to 28g. Therefore, any of the current quality Trap cartridges on the market will prove suitable. There is a case for using a slightly tighter patterning cartridge for the second shot. The second target at Double Trap can sometimes be much further out than a second barrel at Olympic Trap. At these extended ranges pattern quality is at a premium. It might be worth testing different cartridges in your top barrel, choosing one that gives dense, evenly distributed patterns at 40 yards. Use your favourite shot size for the first shot, but, if you favour the smaller sizes of shot, try switching to No.7 (English) for the second. There are cartridges available loaded with extremely hard shot, these are ideal for the second target, provided they print good patterns in your particular gun.

SHOOTING TECHNIQUE

In its original form, Double Trap seemed a sort of amalgamation of Sporting and Trap because of the variable nature of one of the targets. The fact that the targets sometimes crossed made it particularly difficult, and the random nature of this made the whole discipline basically unfair. There was no means of ensuring equality of target distribution. The revised form of the discipline now gives every shooter an equal distribution of targets as is found in Olympic Trap, and Double Trap has now become very much a Trapshooter's game.

STANCE AND HOLD POSITION

The ideal stance is as for the other Trap disciplines. There is no need for any exaggeration in style. Indeed guard against this, as apprehension before the call can create unnecessary tension in the body with disastrous consequences for your timing.

In my experience, the gun muzzles should be held slightly lower on Double Trap to enable you to 'read' the targets better. I personally prefer to hold about 2 to 3ft below the mark, varying the lateral placing of the muzzles according to which stand I am on. (See ABT technique)

Because of the random nature of the targets, a very positive approach must be adopted mentally. Any slight easing off in concentration will result in a miss (or misses). Decide which target you are going to shoot first and concentrate on it. Shoot it quickly and smoothly. When you see it break, switch your attention to the second target and again shoot quickly **AND** smoothly. The same technique as is used for all Trapshooting applies. There is no time for deliberate aiming, the shooting must be smooth and instinctive. Remember to concentrate on that first target. If you don't break the first one you can't kill a pair! Obvious if you think about it.

PROVISIONAL RULES FOR UIT DOUBLE TRAP

The UIT are to be commended for trying to create a new Olympic discipline for shotgun, and they are to be heartily congratulated for altering the format to make the game an equitable and more shootable discipline. The whole basis of Olympic Trap is that all the competitors shoot exactly the same birds, albeit in a different sequence. Now this concept has been applied to Double Trap it has transformed the discipline. The original form might have made a good 'pool' shoot but it was totally inappropriate for an International discipline. The new form of Double Trap has the potential to develop into an exciting and challenging form of clayshooting. Luck should play no part in a test of shooting skill.

The General Technical Rules for all

shooting disciplines and the Special Rules for Clay Target Shooting-Trap (available from the CPSA) apply to this new event unless otherwise specified in the following special regulations.

Double Trap Pit

In an existing Olympic Trap pit, Machines No. 7, 8 and 9 are utilized to shoot Double Trap.

New Double Trap pits can be economically constructed in such a way that the three machines meet the following measurements:

The three machines must be installed in the pit at a maximum distance apart of 1.20m when measured from the pivot points of the throwing arms and when the machines are fixed at 0° angle. The throwing arms of both machines have to be exactly level when both machines are fixed in identical positions. Their distance below ground level, measured at the pivot point of the arm, is a minimum of 50cm and a maximum of 80cm.

Trap No.1 has to be installed to the left, exactly parallel to, and at a right angle to, Machine No.2.

Trap No.2 has to be installed exactly in the middle of the pit directly in front of shooting Station No.3.

Trap No. 3 has to be installed to the right, exactly parallel to, and at a right angle to, Machine No. 2.

The traps must only be released by an electric microphone system in UIT championships and UIT supervised competitions. The release device must guarantee equal distribution of targets to each shooter in a series of 25 doubles. With the correct distribution, in a series of 25 doubles, a shooter will receive two doubles from traps 1 and 2, two doubles from traps 2 and 3, and one double from traps 1 and 3, off each of the five shooting stations.

The five shooting stations must be arranged on a straight line so that Station No.3 (middle position) is exactly at a distance 15m to the rear of the trap pit. The shooters use the same five shooting stations as specified in the General and Special Technical Rules for Trap ranges. The distance between the centres of the shooting stations must measure a minimum of 3.00m and a maximum of 3.30m. (It is likely that the new rules will make provision for 2.5m between stations so that existing Universal Trap layouts may be utilized for shooting Double Trap.)

Target Distances, Angles and Elevations

1 Height

The height of the target path above ground level and at a distance of 10m in front of the throwing point must be 3.5m.

2 Angle

Trap No. 1 (Left hand machine)
The angle is fixed between a minimum of 0° and a maximum of 15° to the LEFT.

Trap No. 2 (Centre machine)

The angle is fixed between 0° and 5° either side of centre.

Trap No. 3 (Right hand machine)

The angle is fixed between a minimum of 0° and a maximum of 15° to the RIGHT.

Distance

The traps shall be adjusted to throw the targets between 55 and 65m. The actual heights, distances and angles will be determined in accordance with the tables in the Clay Target rule book.

Equipment and Ammunition

Guns

All types of shotguns, approved by the Special Technical Rules for Clay Target Shooting. (Art. 4.2.)

Ammunition

Cartridges of 12-gauge or smaller can be used. Shot load must not exceed 28g (loading tolerance of + 0.5g). Pellets must not exceed 2.5mm (+ 0.1mm tolerance).

Conduct of Double Trap

Ready position of the shooter: optional.

Clay Targets

Clay targets must conform with the UIT Special Technical Rules for Clay Target Shooting. For the semi-finals and finals in championship competitions this means 'Flash' targets.

Doubles

A double can only be considered valid when the two clay targets appear simultaneously and undamaged and fly correctly. The decision on the correctness and validity of the doubles is made by the referee.

The result of a double is recorded by two points. If only one target is hit, only one point is recorded. If both targets are hit and broken with one shot the result will be declared 'No bird' and the double repeated.

In the case of an allowable malfunction, a new double has to be thrown.

Individual and Team Event

Squads will normally consist of six shooters.

Start numbers will be drawn at random.

After every double, the shooters rotate according to the Trap rules.

One round consists of 25 doubles (= 50 targets).

International Competition for One Day

Two rounds of 25 doubles for all shooters = 100 targets (also counts as team events for teams of three shooters, shooting 100 targets each).

One round of 25 doubles for the top 24 shooters (semi-final) = 50 targets.

One round of 25 doubles for the top 6 shooters (after 150 targets) = 50 targets.

This gives a result ex 200 targets.

International Competition for Two Days

First Day

Each participant shoots three rounds of 25 doubles = 150 targets.
(Team results for three shooters per team giving team total ex 450 targets.)

Second Day

The top 24 shooters after the first day shoot two rounds of doubles (semi-final) = 100 targets.

The top 6 shooters after 250 targets (first day + semi-final) shoot a final round of 25 doubles giving a final result ex 300 targets.

Tie Breaking

In general:
1. Highest number of doubles broken.
2. Last series (countback).
3. Highest number of hits with the second shot.

After the Finals

1. Highest result of the final round. If there is still a tie for a medal position:

2. 'Sudden death' shoot off on doubles.

3. Each double is considered separately. The participants in the shoot-off have to shoot at the same number of targets and the shoot-off will be conducted for all participants, shooting in turn, on station No.3. at a double thrown off traps 1 and 3.

Team Ties

If two or more teams have the same scores in the first 3 places, ranking must be decided by the combined score of the team members in the last round of 25 doubles, then by the next to last round and so on until the tie is broken.

SKEET SHOOTING

Trapshooting is the original form of clay target shooting. Developed as an inanimate form of live pigeon shooting, it retained much of the format of the live bird sport. Once the clay target had become established, it didn't take long for someone to realize that clays were not only an acceptable substitute for boxed pigeons, but could also be used as simulated game birds to provide practice for field shooting. In an attempt to accomplish this the Davies family from Andover, Massachusetts, developed a form of shooting they named 'shooting round the clock'. As the name implies, the game involved shooting from a number of stands positioned around the perimeter of a circle. The trap was positioned at twelve o'clock in a circle of 25 yards' radius and threw its target directly to six o'clock. The stations corresponded with the hour positions on a clock face, and two targets were taken at each station. This gave 24 targets. As shells come in boxes of 25, the last cartridge was used to take a target from the centre of the circle.

The Davies's developed this game around about the time the First World War was starting, and it remained in this form for a number of years. Then a neighbour of the Davies's started a chicken farm on land adjoining the shooting range and the layout had to be altered to prevent shot dropping on to the unfortunate chickens—shades of some of today's environmental problems facing clay target shooting!

To make the layout safe for the chickens it was decided to place an additional trap at six o'clock and alter the circle into a semi-circle. The same number of targets were retained, but the arc of fire had now been reduced from 360° to 180°. At this stage a friend of the Davies's, William H. Foster, who was editor of the magazines **National Sportsman**, and **Hunting and Fishing**, gave the infant discipline considerable publicity in his two periodicals. The result of this was that many of the readers took up 'clock shooting' and soon Foster was inundated with requests for details as to how the new form of shooting should be set up and conducted. In response to this, Foster drew up a set of rules which were published in both his magazines in early 1926. This was really the beginning of Skeet shooting as we know it today.

Foster realized that 'round the clock' or 'clock shooting' were rather clumsy titles for the new sport, and that a new and shorter name was needed. So he organized a competition in his magazines offering a prize of $100 to the reader who submitted the best name. The response was overwhelming, there being some ten thousand entries received. The honour of renaming 'clock shooting' fell to Mrs Gertrude Hulbert from Montana who submitted the word 'skeet' which is a derivative of an old Scandinavian word meaning 'shoot'. Thus, Charles Davies's invention achieved a name and a set of rules and William H. Foster could truly be said to be 'The Father of Skeet'.

From these early beginnings, Skeet developed rapidly. The first American national Championship took place in Cleveland, Ohio, in 1935. The first European Championship was held in 1954, and in 1968 Skeet was admitted to the Olympic programme at the Mexico Olympics.

It came to Britain in the 1930s and we modified the rules to suit British shooters. The Europeans took up the new discipline and created their own set of rules to make the game much harder than it was originally. Today it is a worldwide sport controlled by three different governing bodies, each with its own distinct set of rules. These governing bodies are the English CPSA who control English (or National) Skeet; the National Skeet Shooting Association who control American Skeet; and the UIT (Union Internationale de Tir) who govern International or Olympic Skeet.

ENGLISH SKEET

The sequence of targets for this discipline have varied over the years. The current sequence is as follows:

TARGET SEQUENCE

Station 1:

High House single

Low House single

Double (High House to be shot first)

Station 2:

High House single

Low House single

Double (High House to be shot first)

Station 3:

High House single

Low House single

Station 4:

High House single

Low House single

Double (the shooter must nominate which target he is taking first, otherwise it will be assumed that the High House target is being taken first)

Station 5:

High House single

Low House single

Station 6:

High House

Low House single

Double (Low House to be shot first)

Station 7:

High House single

Low House single

Double (Low House to be shot first)

This makes a total of 24 targets. If the shooter is still straight at this point, he must shoot either a Low or High House single (his choice) to complete the round of 25 targets. Otherwise the first target missed during the round is repeated, immediately after the miss, to make a total of 25 targets.

Gun Position:
This is optional. The shooter may start with the gun pre-mounted in the shoulder if desired.

Target Speed:
The traps shall be adjusted to throw the target 55 yards in still air conditions.

Gun:
The maximum permitted calibre is 12 gauge.

Cartridge:
From 1 January 1990 the maximum permitted shot charge will be 28g. The maximum permitted shot size is 2mm.

Note: when shooting singles only one cartridge at a time may be loaded into the gun.

AMERICAN (NSSA) SKEET TARGET SEQUENCE

Station 1:

High House single

Low House single

Double (High House to be shot first)

Station 2:

High House single

Low House single

Double (High House to be shot first)

Station 3:

High House single

Low House single

Station 4:

High House single

Low House single

Station 5:

High House single

Low House single

Station 6:

High House single

Low House single

Double (Low House to be shot first)

Station 7:

High House single

Low House single

Double (Low House to be shot first)

Station 8:

High House single

Low House single

This makes 24 targets. As in English Skeet, the first miss is repeated as the twenty-fifth target. If the shooter hits all the 24 targets then the shooter must take a second low house single on Station 8 as his twenty-fifth target.

Gun Position:
Optional. The gun may be pre-mounted into the shoulder if desired.

Target Speed:
The target must travel 60 yards in still air conditions.

Gun:
American Skeet is unique in that there are events held for four different gauges: 12, 20, 28 and .410.

Cartridge: Maximum permitted shot loads:
12 gauge 1 1/8oz
20 gauge 7/8oz
28 gauge 3/4oz
.410 gauge 1/2oz
Shot size: Number 9

OLYMPIC SKEET TARGET SEQUENCE

Station 1:

High House single

Double (High House to be shot first)

Station 2:

High House single

Low House single

Double (High House to be shot first)

Station 3:

High House single

Low house single

Double (High House to be shot first)

Station 4:

High House single

Low House single

Station 5:

High House single

Low House single

Double (Low House to be shot first)

Station 6:

High House single

Low House single

Double (Low House to be shot first)

Station 7:

Double (Low House to be shot first)

Station 8:

High House single

Low House single

This makes a total of 25 targets.

Gun Position:
The toe of the stock must be level with the shooter's hip bone and the shooting jacket must be marked with tape along the waistline to assist refereeing this rule. The targets are subject to a delay of up to 3 seconds and the gun may not be moved until the target appears.

Target Speed:
In calm weather the targets must carry a minimum of 65m and a maximum of 67m.

Gun:
12 gauge is the maximum permitted calibre.

Cartridge:
Maximum permitted shot load: 28 grams (loading tolerance of + 0.5g) The fired case must not exceed 70mm. Pellets must be only spherical in shape, made from lead or lead alloy, and not larger than 2mm in diameter (+0.1mm tolerance). Each round of skeet must be completed with cartridges of one type only.

Note: at UIT Skeet, when shooting singles the shooter MUST load TWO cartridges into the gun (unlike in English Skeet).

ENGLISH SKEET

All of the major gun manufacturers produce models specifically designed for shooting Skeet.

However these are intended primarily for the two eight-station forms of Skeet, UIT and NSSA. In 1977 the English CPSA reverted to the seven station format, omitting the two singles on Station 8, and substituting a double on Station 4. The double on Station 4 caused many English Skeet shooters to re-evaluate their equipment, and in recent years many of the top exponents of this form of shooting have used Sporting guns, often with 30in barrels and a slight degree of choke.

The reasoning behind this is that the longer barrels give greater stability, reducing the tendency to over-lead the slower targets of English Skeet; and a little bit of choke in the top barrel gives greater confidence on the second shot of the double on Station 4. However, the modern purpose built Skeet gun, with 28in barrels, and cylinder or retro choke is perfectly suited to this discipline. Modern Skeet guns tend to be made to full weight, giving good stability of swing, and retro choking, with its elongated shot string will consistently break targets at distances that will amaze you.

The conclusion to be drawn from all this is that any modern Skeet or suitably choked Sporting gun will prove to be satisfactory for the English discipline. Barrel length is dependent on your build and ability to control the gun. My personal preference would be for 28in barrels but if you feel more confident with 30in then by all means use them. Multi-choked guns, with open tubes installed, make an ideal gun with the added advantage that they can double up as Sporting or Game guns, the only proviso being that they are of full weight.

A word of caution here on the subject of Skeet guns. In the early days of Skeet, some manufacturers offered what their publicity departments described as 'Skeet guns'. These generally had 26in barrels and were basically modified field guns. The combination of short barrels and light weight made for fast handling guns, too fast for consistent shooting at any of the Skeet disciplines. You may be offered one of these old guns at a bargain price; they make super fast handling game guns for relatively close range shooting but if serious Skeet shooting is your aim, then avoid them!

THE CARTRIDGE

From 1 January 1990 the maximum permitted shot load for English Skeet has been 28g, which is a reduction of 4g on the previous maximum load. This sounds a lot, but in fact should make no difference to the level of scores in English Skeet. The lighter load has been mandatory for UIT (Olympic) Skeet for the 1989 season and the leading scores at major championships worldwide have not suffered any reduction at all. If 28g can cope with the fiercer targets of the international discipline, there is no doubt that it will prove more than adequate for English Skeet. The only problem that can arise is a psychological one. If you believe that the reduction in the shot load will adversely affect your shooting, then it will. In practice, there is no reason why your scores should suffer—indeed the lack of recoil of the lighter load may well improve your scores. Therefore select with confidence any good proprietary Skeet cartridge loaded with 2mm shot.

TECHNIQUE

English Skeet provides an ideal discipline for the novice clayshooter to develop his skills. It provides the beginner with the opportunity to shoot a wide variety of single and double targets at relatively short range. Whilst the targets are not intimidating, they present quite a challenge to the person who wishes to master this form of shooting.

In many respects, English Skeet is the perfect discipline for the beginner. Learning to shoot it properly and practising it will lay the foundation of good gun handling, which will stand the novice in good stead whatever form of clayshooting (including the Trap disciplines) he ultimately aspires to. The first formal clayshooting that I took part in was English Skeet, and those weekly sessions at the Belfry Gun Club (now unfortunately closed in favour of a golf course), helped me develop a basic framework of shooting skills which have proved to be of great benefit in all forms of clay-shooting.

You only have to see some of the appalling styles in use at Trap shoots to realize many trapshooters never learn proper gun-mounting. Time spent shooting English Skeet at the start of a shooter's career can save a lot of frustration later on.

You will have noticed, in the resumé of the format for this type of shooting that the gun position is optional, permitting a shooter to call for his target(s) with the gun already pre-mounted in the shoulder. Obviously, your gun-handling will not derive much benefit from shooting English Skeet if you start with the gun already in the shoulder. Fortunately, all forms of Skeet are better shot with the gun held out of the shoulder until the target appears, improving your all-round shooting skills.

STANCE

The ideal stance for English Skeet is similiar to that used for Sporting. The feet are slightly spread with the toes of the leading foot pointed towards the point where you expect to break the target. The body weight is biassed slightly on to the front foot. The heel of the stock is tucked under the armpit and the muzzles held on the line of the target flightpath.

Station by Station

Station 1

High House single
The gun and leading foot are pointed towards the target crossing point. The muzzles are then lifted to a position just over half-way back towards the High House. Raise the eyes to look for the target about half-way between the gun and the target opening. Concentrate. Call for the target. The eyes lock on to the clay as the left hand pushes the muzzles into the target. As the stock slides into the shoulder the trigger is pulled.

Low House single
This is an incoming target reminiscent of a low driven sporting bird. The muzzles are held about half-way between the Low House and the target crossing point. The eyes are turned towards the Low House ready to pick up the clay as it appears. As the target emerges the eyes lock on to it, the left hand pushes the

muzzles on to the clay and and moves with it. As the gun accelerates past the target the trigger is pulled.

Double

The first bird is shot in exactly the same manner as the single. After the trigger is pulled on the High House bird the eyes and muzzle switch to the second target, locking on to it, accelerating past it, and delivering the shot. A vital point when shooting doubles is that it is impossible to kill the pair if the first target is missed. This sounds obvious, but is amazing how many people miss because they try to look at both targets at once. Concentrate on that first target, and only move to the second bird AFTER you have fired at the first. The danger is that, if your attention wanders to the second bird before you have completed your first shot, then your gun swing will stop, resulting in a miss behind.

Station 2

High House single

The target on this station presents more of a quartering shot. Line up the feet and gun with the target crossing point and bring the muzzles back to a point about one-third of the way out from the High House, on the line of target flight. The eyes then turn back a little bit further towards the house. When the target emerges, the eyes lock on to it, the left hand pushes the muzzles on to flightpath and as the

barrels accelerate past the target, the shot is fired.

Low House single

The gun is held about half-way out towards the crossing point from the house. The eyes look back to where you can best pick up the target. As the target the eyes lock on, the pushes the muzzles after the eyes, as the target, eyes and muzzles converge the gun is accelerated past the target and the trigger pulled.

Double

Shoot the High House target as you did the single. AFTER the shot is completed, switch your eyes and muzzles to the second bird, accelerate past it and complete the shot.

Station 3

High House

Face the target crossing point and turn the gun back towards the High House. The muzzles should be held at a point that enables you to mount the gun on to the target without rushing. As this target is more of a crossing shot, a little bit of experimentation during practice to establish the best hold position for you will prove beneficial. You should be able to mount the gun smoothly into the shoulder without any apparent rush. Take the eyes back towards the trap house. Concentrate. Call the target. See it, put the muzzles on it, accelerate past it and fire.

Low House

Hold the gun half-way between the Low House and the crossing point. Look back towards the trap. When the target appears, lock on to it, accelerate the muzzles past it and pull the trigger. Remember to keep the gun swinging and follow through after the shot. Any tendency to stop the gun as you fire will have a fatal effect on your score.

Station 4

This is the bogey stand for many Skeet shooters. The singles present little difficulty but the thought of the double sends some shooters into total panic. There is no need for this: you have considerably more time than you think in which to deal with the double. If you don't believe me, find an Olympic (ISU) Skeet layout and try the doubles on Stations 3 and 5. Now that is fast! You might even try a double off 4 on an ISU field. When you return to an English layout the Station 4 double will seem a lot less intimidating.

High House single

The gun hold position is on the flightline about one third of the way out from the High House towards the target crossing point. This is a crossing target but don't think in terms of deliberate lead. If you try to measure precise forward allowance on targets it stifles the natural reactions of your body, induces hesitation and causes the swing to falter.

Pick up the target with your eyes. The left hand pushes the gun on to the clay, and as the eyes, muzzles and target all converge, the stock slips into the shoulder. The gun accelerates past the bird and the shot is fired. You won't have to think about lead — your instinctive timing will ensure that the trigger is pulled at the right moment.

Low House single

The technique here is the same as for the High House only in the other direction! Again, guard against trying to make conscious allowances for lead. Let your natural timing do most of the work for you.

Double

This is where the panic sets in. Don't let it—there is no need. On Station 4 the choice of which target you shoot first is up to you. When preparing to call for the pair you must nominate to the referee whether you intend to shoot the High House or Low House target first. Set yourself up for your nominated target and when it emerges, shoot it in exactly the same way as the single. When the shot is fired, switch your attention to the second bird. Eyes and muzzles should lock on to it as the gun is swung past it, the trigger is pulled and the follow through completed. The result should be pair killed.

Don't be panicked by these targets. Watch some of the top English Skeet shooters in action, such as Andy Harvison or Martin Elworthy, they

never seem rushed when they are shooting well. If you keep your head you will find no difficulty in dealing with this double. A great many targets are missed here because the shooter has talked himself out of it before he has even loaded the gun, so, don't be a defeatist—be confident and decisive in your approach and be successful.

In the question of which target to take first on the double, many English Skeet shooters seem to favour shooting the High House target first. My personal preference is to shoot the Low House bird first. As a right-handed shooter, I find that my easiest swing is to the left and this enables me to shoot the Low House (right to left) bird a little bit quicker without losing any control. Also, the High House target seems to have a flatter trajectory, making it easier to shoot when past the centre point.

I feel that anyone taking up English Skeet should experiment on this double in practice. Find out which way round feels more comfortable to you. It can be an advantage to be able to alternate which target you take first; in bad weather conditions, one target may be affected more than the other. This is the one to take first if the weather is conspiring to ruin your score.

Top English skeet shooter Martin Elworthy, about to shoot Low 5.

Station 5

High House single

This target is now presented as an incomer. Aim to shoot it just past the centre and resist the temptation to ride it down the range and make sure of it. Hold the gun half way between the High House and crossing point. Pick up the clay with your eyes, push the muzzles on to it, accelerate past it and shoot.

Low House

This target requires a positive approach. It should be shot the instant the gun passes it. Any attempt to ride it out usually results in a loss. Hold the muzzles about half-way out from the Low House. Look back towards the target opening. Concentrate. Call. As your eyes, the muzzles and the target converge, pull the trigger with the gun still accelerating.

Station 6

High House single

The hold position is with the gun about a third of the way out from the High House towards the centre. Look back towards the target opening. This target should be broken just after it crosses the centre of the range. This is another target that tempts you into being too deliberate. Watch out for this. The stilted swing of someone trying to make sure is rarely successful.

Low House single

The gun is held half-way out from the

Low House towards the target crossing point. As with Station 5 the shot is made as the eyes, muzzles and target converge, with your swing accelerating the gun past the clay.

Double

After Station 4. you will find that on the doubles, the Low House target is shot first. Shoot the Low House target in exactly the same way as you shot the single. This will leave you with plenty of time to switch to the High House target, swing past it and annihilate it.

Station 7

Nearly finished, one more station to go. Station 7 targets are somewhat easier than the preceding stands and with the round almost concluded it is very easy to relax a bit when coming to this stand. This is not to be recommended: that slight easing up can cost you targets. Every bird on the layout demands maximum concentration if you are to shoot a winning score. Some years ago, top GB Skeet shooter, Joe Neville missed Low 7 for a 200 straight at an ISU Skeet selection shoot. As he gazed ruefully at his 199 on the scoreboard, Joe was heard to mutter something about there being no easy targets! So give Station 7 your maximum effort. The High House target should cause few problems being ˌa relatively straightforward incomer, but the Low House is easily missed if you get sloppy on it.

High House single

Although this is a straightforward incoming target, it is again important to guard against being too deliberate. The target should be broken about half-way between the centre peg and the low house.

Low House single

Hold the muzzles on the flightpath of the target, with your eyes looking about half-way to the centre peg. As the target comes into your vision, push the muzzles 'into' the target and pull the trigger as the stock hits your shoulder. You must attack this target as an aggressive approach will eliminate any tendency to hesitate; but don't let your aggression destroy the smoothness of your gun-mounting.

Double

The first (Low House) target is shot in precisely the same manner as the single. This will give you plenty of time to switch to the incoming (High House) bird, pull through it and vaporize it!

The Optional or Repeat Target

There is still one target unaccounted for to complete a round of 25. If you have the misfortune to miss a target during the round, you will be required to repeat that first miss immediately. This probably seems a bit nasty. Having missed a target, and suffered a blow to your confidence, you are then compelled to have another go at missing it! This is what many people actually do. They call for the repeat, still thinking about the lost bird, and promptly miss again. The secret here is to pause for a second, compose yourself, forget the lost bird and concentrate on the repeat. When the target appears, lock on to it, shoot decisively and smoke it! There, that'll teach it to escape in the first place!

If you have the good fortune to complete the first 24 targets without a miss, then you will be required to take an optional target to complete the round of 25. In the old days, shooters were permitted to opt for any one of the single targets but this caused some delay as people wandered from stand to stand to complete their round. Under the current rules, you have a choice of either of the singles on Station 7. Choose whichever you prefer, but give it maximum concentration and effort. Remember, you haven't shot 25 straight until you break that last target. A momentary lapse of concentration will leave you looking at a 24 and thinking of what might have been.

One final point, when shooting Skeet wear shooting glasses with impact resistant lenses. These will protect your eyes from pieces of broken target, particularly on Stations 1 and 7. Glasses just might save your eyesight!

AMERICAN (NSSA) SKEET

The technique for English Skeet will work equally well for NSSA Skeet,

the only difference being that there is no double on Station 4. Instead there are two singles on Station 8. A modification of ISU technique will enable you to deal with those targets off the centre peg.

OLYMPIC SKEET

This is the game played at international level, and as its name implies it is part of the Olympic programme. ISU Skeet, Olympic Trap and FITASC Sporting are the Blue Riband events of clay target shooting. ISU Skeet is a demanding and challenging form of shooting that tests shooting skill to its utmost. I frequently shoot this discipline in training for Olympic Trap as I find there are sound lessons in gun-handling to be learnt at ISU Skeet that can prove very beneficial to the trapshooter. Firstly it places a premium on good gun-mounting. Secondly, the 0-3 second delay teaches the shooter not to move the gun before the target appears, and, most importantly, it demands a fast, responsive gun swing.

I have always shot ISU Skeet with a variation of the 'swing-through' technique, but there is another way of shooting it. This is known as 'sustained lead', and it is the method employed by the majority of the current winners on the international circuit. This is not to say that 'swing-through' is not successful—Wally Sykes used the swing-through method to great effect over many years in the

British team—but 'sustained lead' is the chosen method of many of todays champions.

Because I do not use this method to shoot ISU Skeet, I am indebted to my good friend Paul Bentley for his help with the following section. Paul has been one of our most successful ISU shooters over the past decade and is a good advertisement for the effectiveness of the sustained lead method. His successes include European and Commonwealth medals as well as many British titles.

ISU SKEET

There are two disciplines of clay-shooting in the Olympic programme,

ISU Skeet and Olympic Trap. The two disciplines differ completely in format and shooting technique. Because of the unpredictability of its targets, Olympic Trap is a mixture of technique and a heavy dose of pure reflex; whereas ISU Skeet demands a marked degree of studied application, with less emphasis on the reflexes— although this may not be apparent to the beginner.

A reliance on reflex-only shooting does work at ISU Skeet, but the methodical shooter, who pays particular attention to technique, will usually produce more consistent scores.

Anyone unfamiliar with ISU Skeet,

The relaxed style of French shooter, Stefan Tayssier.

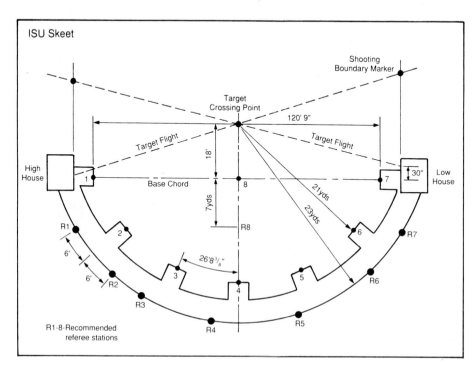

reading what follows, might be forgiven for thinking that it sounds a bit like robotic computer programming. In fact that is almost what it is. It has been said that a monkey of average intelligence could be taught to shoot ISU Skeet, and while that might be taking things a bit far, it is certainly true that a shooter can be programmed to shoot this discipline.

For all that, ISU Skeet remains one of the most challenging of the clay disciplines, all the more so, because, unlike the Trap disciplines, there is no worthwhile base on which to cut ISU teeth. Since the CPSA and the ISU amended their respective rules in the late seventies, the change from English to ISU Skeet is so drastic as to cause many novices to give up at the first attempt. This is a pity, because with a bit of effort it is quite possible to shoot the same scores at ISU as one previously shot at the domestic version, with the added incentive of the possibility of qualifying for a British team to compete at international level.

The ISU Skeet Gun

As stated, many English Skeet shooters use their Sporting guns to deadly effect, but for anyone contemplating a serious attempt at the international version a more specialized shotgun is recommended.

Chokes and barrel length

Whilst some very good English Skeet shooters achieve great success using guns with a fair degree of choke, this can prove to be a very definite handicap when shooting the ISU version. Within the bounds of consistency, the wider the pattern the better. Even at the highest level of competition, chipped targets play an important part in compiling a decent score, and many major titles have been won by a competitor who chipped his way round the last 25 targets. Any substantial degree of choke would not have collected these vital chips. The restricted pattern would have missed the target altogether. Many of the specialist skeet guns available today have retro or 'Tula' chokes and these have proved very successful in producing high scores. Anyone who doubts their effectiveness should examine the results of the Russian team over the last 20 years. To a man, they all use retro-choked guns.

Barrel length, allied to weight distribution, has a marked effect on gun-handling. A good ISU Skeet gun will be fractionally muzzle heavy and, therefore, will not need great length to provide stability and momentum of swing. 26½in barrels may seem short but in guns weighing around 8lbs prove very effective. Certainly 28in barrels are the longest worth considering. All the Continental manufacturers who make specialist ISU Skeet guns supply them with barrels that fall within these parameters. As has been said in the English Skeet section, avoid the old fashioned short barrelled, light-weight Skeet guns which are far too light to be controllable at ISU Skeet.

Stocks

The stock-on-the-hip ready position required in ISU Skeet forces the shooter to mount the gun with a very apparent lifting motion of the right hand and this movement tends to cause the muzzles to dip and the shot to go low. To compensate for this many top international shooters have their guns stocked with high combs, similiar to Trap gun comb height.

High stocks come in two types; the straight combed and the Monte Carlo, the latter being of particular use to the person who adopts a very upright stance and wishes to avoid dropping his head down to meet the stock.

A shorter than usual stock is also advantageous as it makes gun-mounting easier. Don't take this to extremes though: ¼in less than the appropriate Sporting stock measurement is about right. It is a good idea to fit a rubber pad to assist in locating the gun once it's mounted, and to prevent it slipping as the shot is fired. To prevent the pad snagging on the shooting vest during gun-mounting, tape or varnish the sides. Electricians' plastic tape is ideal for this purpose.

The pistol grips on most under and overs these days are massive and unwieldy affairs, often made worse by the addition of so-called anatomical bulges. These actually defeat their own purpose, i.e. to provide a tension free grip which nevertheless maintains full and easy control of the back end of the gun. If the thumb and fingers cannot unite with ease around the grip, then proper control is inhibited. The comfort of a pistol grip is a matter of personal preference, but, as it has a profound effect on the gun control it is worth spending time getting it right.

Trigger pulls

3½ to 4 lbs is about right for most people, but it is more important that the triggers should break crisply. Consistent shooting is not easy with sloppy, spongy trigger pulls. It is well worth spending money to have them adjusted properly by an expert. Once they are adjusted, check them regularly as all things mechanical can alter with use.

The ready position

A point which even quite experienced ISU Skeet shooters get wrong is the mandatory 'ready' position, and this

can cause arguments when shooting at home and real problems when shooting in International competitions. Get it right from the start and avoid the hassle. Done properly, the stock must touch the crest of the hip bone and remain there until the target emerges. It is not sufficient just to have the stock level with the hip-bone, the ISU rules require that the gunstock is in CONTACT with the body.

TECHNIQUE

The following is based on the 'sustained lead' technique, although certain targets must be shot 'swing-through' style. This combination of two quite different techniques is really only possible for someone who has a good grounding in the 'swing-through' method and is not rec-ommended for newcomers to shotgun shooting. Generally speaking, only the second targets on the doubles are shot using the swing-through style; some because there is no other way, while others are shot this way to avoid confusion in an already complex method. At international level the majority of competitors use this combination of methods.

With the 'sustained-lead' system, in the initial stages of the swing, the muzzles are pointing a long way in front of the target. This will alter rapidly as the target nearly catches the accelerating muzzles. The target must not be allowed to catch the muzzles, however, and with practice the shooter will soon learn to move the gun at the speed required to maintain the necessary forward allowance.

The feet should be no more than a shoulder width apart, preferably less.

A blight in the lives of most beginners is the random 0-3 second delay in the target release. Being unsure of exactly when the target is going to emerge makes many shooters rely on the sound of the trap firing to warn them of the target's launch. Don't adopt this habit; if you do, every slight sound will set the muzzles twitching and when the target does appear, a horrible, slashing snap shot is the result. Learn to react only to the sight of the target, then your eyes will be controlling every-thing, the basis for all good shooting.

Finally, on the subject of general technique, all shots to the left or right entail a turn of the whole body. It is not just an arm and hand movement. The ability to master these targets can be greatly improved by regular periods of 'dry' practice away from the skeet field.

Station by Station

Station 1

Before shooting the first round of the competition the squad is allowed to view a target from each house, just to make sure that the targets are going where they are supposed to. Check to see if the targets are dipping or climbing, or wandering off

Former Grand Prix of Europe winner, Jim Sheffield, showing an easy, relaxed style. Note ISU gun position.

regulation position, the barrels should be elevated so that they are about 40° to the ground and be pointing along the same line as the targets are flying (remembering that this is not necessarily over the centre peg!). Stations 1 and 7 are the only time the shooter is looking directly over the barrels for the target. Focus can be a problem here and it's important to look out just above and beyond the muzzles so that the eyes do not become focused on the gun. If this happens the target will emerge as a blur and will probably remain one as it flies on unscathed!

Call for the target only when you are ready. Make sure that the concentration is directed at seeing that target. Many shooters call whilst still shuffling their feet into position. If the random delay mechanism decides it's time for an instant release, they can literally be caught out on the wrong foot, unprepared to tackle the target. When you call 'pull' you should be fully prepared and mean it.

The high target is a simple going away shot that appears to be heading slightly downhill. The technique is to point the muzzles straight at it while smoothly bringing the stock to the face. A violent heave into the cheek is definitely out, since it will probably hurt and it causes the muzzles to dip below the target. Ideally, the muzzles should be slightly under the target throughout the mounting movement, the trigger being pulled as the gun beds firmly into the face and shoulder.

line. On some layouts targets can be all over the place and it's important to have a good look to ensure you don't get taken by surprise. A trap which throws a target consistently off line is not a problem, unless the deviation is extreme. The tricky ones are those that vary from target to target, and these must be watched carefully. Unfortunately a new ruling by the ISU does not permit this opportunity to view the targets on the second, or subsequent rounds.

High House single
Your weight should be slightly on your leading foot. With the gun in the

Double

Once the high target has been mastered, the double presents no problems. In the double it is essential that the first target, from the High House, is shot in exactly the same way as the single. Performed correctly, the target will be broken three to five yards before the centre peg (target crossing point). There is no rush to switch to the second target, which will appear to the left of the gun just after the high target is broken. This target needs a lead of no more than a foot, and, without removing the gun from the shoulder, the swing is reversed, the target swung through and the shot is fired with the target about midway between the centre peg and the High House.

Station 2

High House single

This is the first of the more difficult targets and causes more than its fair share of problems to novice Skeet shooters. There are several important factors which must be right if this target is to be dealt with effectively and with confidence.

The first is stance. The foot position should be with the leading foot pointing to where you intend to break the target, ie around the centre of the layout. It's tempting to turn the body more towards the Low House, but this is self-defeating as it throws too much emphasis on arm and hand movement and hinders the shot being

achieved with a body turn. Once again the the weight should just be favouring the leading foot.

The second factor is muzzle position. Most top shooters have the muzzles pointing to the right of parallel with the face of the High House. The muzzle height should be such that, from the shooter's point of view, the muzzles are slightly below the flight line of the target. Of course, the muzzles are actually pointing considerably higher than this.

The third factor is looking for the target in the right spot. Some excellent Skeet shooters look right back to the target opening. These are the exception, though, and most shooters will benefit from looking for the target midway between the house and the muzzles. This helps maintain a good head position, whereas turning right back to the house turns the head away from the gun. Looking back to the house can also result in the target appearing as a blur which never really resolves into sharp focus.

The final hurdle is timing. Not the timing of the shot but the timing of the start of the swing. The swing must start as soon as the target appears in the shooter's peripheral vision. The target is to be shot 'sustained lead' and this requires that the shooter gets the gun in motion as soon as the target appears. This entails pushing the barrels to the right at the same time as the gun is being brought smoothly to the shoulder. The degree of 'push' to the right must be

118

adjusted to match the speed of the target, which, contrary to first impressions, is not that quick. The 'push' must be just enough to keep the muzzles pointing about a foot ahead of the target so that, when the gun is firmly located in the shoulder, the shot can be instantly fired. Given reasonable reflexes, the target will be broken a yard or two before it reaches the centre peg. There is no time for re-alignment on this shot. Once the target is on its way you are committed. Right or wrong, fire without hesitation. Whilst a shot that is not quite right may well connect if you fire at the first attempt, hanging about and trying to 'make sure' will result in a zero on the scoreboard. Undoubtedly the old adage about 'he who hesitates. . . .' applies one 100 per cent to this target.

Low House single

An easier target than the previous one, nevertheless this bird demands full attention. Any slight lapse in concentration can see this target sailing on intact.

The stance and weight distribution are similar to those for the High House target. The muzzles should be pointed over Station 8 and held just below the anticipated flightpath of the target. There is no need to rush this target. Immediately the target emerges the gun-mount and swing should gently commence, the lead being adjusted to about 2½ft. It is not necessary to fire the instant the

gun hits the shoulder: many shooters prefer to allow the target to come in a bit first. This must not be taken to extremes and the shot must still be taken by reflex, any tendency to take deliberate aim being avoided. A good follow through is essential.

Double

The high target is taken exactly the same as the single. There must be no attempt to look for the second target until the first has been dealt with. Once this has been done the eyes will pick up the second bird just to the left of the muzzles. The muscular tension is eased slightly as the swing is reversed but the gun is kept fully mounted. This second target is shot swing-through style, the muzzles being moved through the target and the shot fired when the lead is correct. As on the single, a good follow through is a must.

Station 3

High House single

One of the supreme tests of sound technique, this target lends itself perfectly to the sustained lead method of shooting. Basic stance and weight distribution are as for Station 2, the muzzles again being held just below the target flightpath. The barrels should be pointed directionally in such a way that the shooter has to react the instant the target appears. Too far out slows the timing and results in the target getting well downrange before the shot is fired.

119

World and Olympic champion, Matt Dryke, showing his crouched style of skeet shooting. His record proves its effectiveness.

House target, except the barrels are pointed midway between the Low House and the centre peg. The muzzles are held just below the target flightpath. Look for the target to the left of the target opening, just beyond the house. Call, and as the target emerges the muzzles move off ahead of it. The stock moves smoothly to the face and shoulder, a lead of about 4ft is seen, and the shot is fired. The follow through is continued down the range after the trigger is pulled. The target will break three to four yards past the centre peg.

Double

The first (High House) target is simply a repeat of the single, utilizing exactly the same timing. As the shot is completed at the High House target, the second bird will be seen just to the left of the muzzles, racing in the opposite direction. The swing is reversed, the muzzles are swung through the target, as the correct lead is seen the shot is fired. It is important to maintain the follow through on this shot to eliminate any tendency to stop the swing at the moment of firing.

Station 4

High House single

Stance and balance are as for the previous stations. The barrels are pointed midway between the High House and the centre peg with the muzzles just below the target flight-path. Look for the target just outside

Too close in lets the target pass the muzzles, leaving the shooter struggling to catch up. Experiment to establish the best position, initially starting with the barrels pointing midway between the High House and the centre peg, adjusting this until the correct place for the individual is found.

Look just to the right of the target opening. The instant the target appears the muzzles begin moving ahead of it and the gun-mounting commences. Ideally the gun contacts firmly to the face and shoulder with an established lead of 3 to 4 feet. Fire and follow through, the target will break just before or over the centre peg.

Low House single

The set up position is as for the High

the edge of the house. As the target appears the swing commences so that the muzzles are kept ahead throughout. As the gun is swung and mounted the lead is adjusted to about 4ft, and as the stock makes firm contact with the face and shoulder, the shot is fired. It is essential to maintain the follow through well after the shot is taken.

Low House single

The barrels are pointed midway between the centre peg and the Low House with the muzzles held just below the target flightpath. The eyes look for the clay just outside the house. As it appears, the swing and gun-mounting commence with the muzzles moving off ahead of the target. The stock meets the face and shoulder, the lead is adjusted to about 4ft and the shot fired, with the gun continuing to follow through. The target will break just beyond the centre peg.

Station 5

High House single

The stance is as for previous stations. The barrels are pointed midway between the High House and the centre peg with the muzzle just below the flightpath of the target. The eyes are held just outside the High House target opening. The instant the target appears the barrels start moving, keeping the muzzles ahead throughout the shot. As the gun mounts into the shoulder the

lead is adjusted to around 4ft and the shot taken. Follow through and don't be tempted to ride this this one down the range.

Low House single

This is a frequently missed target! Stance is the same as for the High House. The muzzles are held below the target flightpath about midway between target crossing point and the Low House. Look just forward of the house, level with the target opening. Concentrate, then call. Move quickly and smoothly with the barrels ahead of the target, adjust the lead to about 3½ft as the gun is sliding into the shoulder. Don't hesitate, fire, following through down the range.

Double

The first target (Low House) is simply a repeat of the single with one slight

Another 'croucher', Cuban shooter Rodriguez.

modification. The follow through must be curtailed and the swing reversed the instant the target breaks. The second (High House) target must be attacked in a decisive manner in order to catch it, swing through and kill it. The lead will be 4-5ft and following through after the shot is vital.

Station 6

High House single

This is a relatively easy target, and the round is nearing completion. Guard against complacency. A lapse of concentration at this stage can knock big holes in a score.

Stance is as previously. The barrels point over the centre station with the muzzles held just below the flightpath of the target. Look just ahead of the target opening and as the clay appears the muzzles move smoothly ahead of it as the gun slides to the shoulder. The lead is adjusted to about 2½ft as the gun beds into the shoulder, and the shot is fired as you maintain this lead in front of the target, following through after the trigger is pulled.

Low House single

Hold the barrels slightly to the left of the traphouse, with the muzzles a little below the target's flightpath. The eyes must look at a point where the target can first be seen clearly. This will vary from shooter to shooter and a certain amount of experimentation will be necessary to establish

the ideal position. As the target emerges the muzzles must stay ahead of it as the gun-mounting is completed. This target needs relatively little lead, around a foot is adequate. As the stock makes contact the shot is fired.

Double

The first bird (Low House) is a repeat of the single. As the target breaks the second bird will be seen just to the right of the muzzles. The swing is reversed, the muzzles overtaking the target, 2½ft of lead is seen and the shot fired.

Station 7

Double

As you will have seen from the resumé of Skeet disciplines earlier in the chapter, there are no singles on Station 7: just a straightforward double. So straightforward that even the best of shots have been known to make a mess of it occasionally!

Guard against being slapdash on these targets. The round is nearly over and this pair should be a gift, but if the concentration falters, or carelessness creeps in zeros appear on the scoreboard.

The gun is held with the barrels pointed along the flightline of the Low House target. The muzzles are held so that the target appears just above them. The gun is pointed straight at the target as it comes into view and the trigger pulled as the stock makes firm contact with the face and shoulder. Don't hesitate on this one. As the target breaks, the muzzles will be pointing ahead of the second (High House) target. The swing is reversed, a lead of about 18in maintained ahead of the clay, and the shot is delivered about half-way between the crossing point and the Low House. Keep swinging until the target breaks.

Station 8

High House single

The muzzles are held level with the target opening and about 6-7ft to the right of it. The eyes look just to the right of the target opening. As the target appears, the muzzles start moving ahead of it as the stock starts sliding to the shoulder. At the instant the gun is mounted the shot is fired, the momentum of the barrels causing the gun to follow through. Constant practice at the outset is the secret to this one. The more times it is shot, the quicker the target will be seen.

Low House single

The last target of the round. Concentrate. The muzzles are held level with the target opening 6-7ft out from the edge of the traphouse. Look for the target just to the left of the target opening. Concentrate on ident-

A tough man to beat! Russian shooter Timokhin moves on to a target.

ifying it the moment it appears. The barrels move the instant the target appears and stay ahead of the clay as the gun is mounted. As the gun beds in to the shoulder, the trigger is pulled. Again the momentum of the gun on this fast, close target, will maintain the follow through.

Both these targets demand a high level of commitment. There is no time for correction so be fully prepared before calling and attack them smoothly and positively.

THE OLYMPIC FORMAT

After the 1984 Olympics the UIT (ISU) came under intense pressure from the International Olympic Committee (IOC) to find a means of making the shooting sports more appealing to television and spectators. This caused much headscratching as the UIT is not just responsible for Olympic shotgun disciplines, but is also the governing body for the Olympic rifle and pistol events. Clay target shooting has plenty of instant action and already had quite an element of visual appeal: the result of the shot can be seen instantly and scoring is of a hit or miss nature, so it is easy for the crowd to follow. Watching rifle and pistol shooting, on the other hand, is about as exciting as watching grass grow to the uninformed spectator. This is not to denigrate the disciplines of precision shooting. The rifle and pistol disciplines, as represented in the Olympic programme, are among the most exacting sports in the world, and the leading competitors are amongst the most dedicated sportsmen and women I have ever met; but their sport is not visually appealing.

So the UIT had the problem of coming up with a competition format that would increase the appeal of both clay target and precision shooting. Their answer was to introduce a Final into the programme of all competitions. After the normal course of fire has been concluded at Trap and Skeet, the top six shooters are required to shoot a further round of 25 targets which is added to the 200 bird score to give a total ex 225 targets to decide the medal positions. This Final round is to conducted on 'Flash' targets to increase the visual appeal. (A 'Flash' target is the same size and colour as a standard clay pigeon, but has an insert of coloured powder that is released when the target is broken producing a spectacular cloud of coloured dust in the sky.)

All Olympic, World, Continental and other events run under the auspices of the UIT have to be conducted under these rules.

The competitions are now run as follows:

● All competitors shoot the first 150 targets over the first two days (75 each day).

● On the third day the top 24 competitors (after 150 targets) shoot a further 50 targets. This gives them a result ex 200.

● The top 6 competitors (ex 200) shoot a further series of 25 targets (using 'Flash' clays) to decide the first 6 placings ex 225 targets.

● If there is a tie for inclusion in the top 24 (Semi-final) or the top 6 (Final) then the normal UIT rules on 'count-back' apply.

● If there are tied scores after the Final round the following rules apply:

1. The decision is based on the highest score in the Final (ex 25).

2. In the case of equal scores ex 225 and equal scores in the Final (ex 25) then the shooters who are tied continue to shoot on a 'sudden death' basis.

(i) Trap
Each tied shooter shoots station after station in sequence until a 'lost' target is registered. Each shooter must shoot at the same number of stations and targets.

(ii) Skeet
Each shooter must shoot on the same stations and targets specified for that station. The shooter who hits the least number of targets on the respective station is the loser. That is how major championships are decided. There are certain elements of this new system that are less than

satisfactory. It is possible (and has happened) that a shooter can lead the competition over 200 targets with, say, a score of 199. There could be three shooters just behind him on 198. If they all shoot 25 in the final and the guy on 199 shoots 24, then all four would be equal ex 225. Unfortunately, the shooter with 199 +24 would be eliminated from the medals although his total equals the three shooters with 198 + 25. Those three will continue to shoot 'sudden death' until a result is established.

To me this seems more than a little unfair, and I feel that it is something the UIT would do well to re-examine. Equal scores are equal scores regardless of the sequence in which they were shot. The amount of time saved at the end of competition by the present rules is negligible and the present situation detracts from the fairness of the event.

OLYMPIC QUALIFICATION

The International Olympic Committee also required of the UIT that they introduce a system of qualification that would reduce the number of shooting competitors at the Olympic Games, and at the same time result in an increase in the standard of the competitors. This has led to the introduction of a Quota system of Olympic places, and a Minimum Qualifying Score to become eligible to take part in the Olympic competition.

The Quota System

Prior to 1984 there were two places available to each country in both the Olympic disciplines (Trap and Skeet). The new rules have removed those automatic places and now each country must attempt to win places for their shooters by competing in specified events in the run up to the games. These events include World Cups (where there is one Olympic place for the winner) and World and Continental Championships (where there might be up to six places avalable). Each individual shooter can only win one place for his country and each country can win a maximum of three places. It is important to note that the shooter wins the Olympic place for his country, not for himself. This new arrangement severely curtailed the number of contestants at the Seoul Olympics. Many of the stronger shooting countries ended up with three shooters, where some of the smaller ones didn't get to shoot at all. All this is somewhat contrary to the Olympic ethos. Great Britain, unfortunately, only managed to win one place, at Olympic Trap. Fortunately there is a system of 'wild cards', given at the discretion of the President of UIT, which can give places to those countries that come very close to getting a Quota Place but don't quite make it. Under this system, Great Britain received a place in Skeet. So, our team in the 1988 Olympics was reduced to half strength by the imposition of these new rules.

The Minimum Qualifying Score

In order to ensure that people taking part in the Games are of a suitable standard of skill for Olympic participation, a Minimum Qualifying Score was introduced after 1984. This was 188 ex 200 in both Trap and Skeet. This score had to be obtained at designated events prior to the Games (World Cups, Continental and World Championships). For the 1992 Olympics this MQS has been reduced to 182 for Trap and 184 for Skeet.

This has been a fairly drastic response, by the UIT, to the IOC's demands. Although, I am sure that the UIT made these changes with the best of intentions, I feel that they haven't quite got it right and that the alterations may prove damaging to the sport in the long run by reducing the chances of participation, which could result in a reduction in interest by both competitor and country alike.

COMPETITION PREPARATION

Success at any competitive sport is not just determined by ability. In order to give yourself the best chance of success in competition, it is vital that you are one hundred per cent prepared before the match commences. This preparation starts well before you arrive at the shooting ground and your approach will obviously depend on the discipline and the duration of the competition.

Obviously, a very important part of preparation is to be suitably equipped. A shooter can take part in a competition with only two basic pieces of equipment—a suitable gun and the appropriate cartridges. However there are a number of 'extras' which can make competing much easier and also make the sport a lot more comfortable and safe.

ACCESSORIES

The Shooting Jacket

A shooting vest is the ideal garment for the competition shooter. It should have roomy pockets, large enough to hold the cartridges you require for a round. There should be a leather shoulder pad, which is securely stitched and wrinkle free. If you are primarily a Trapshooter the shoulder pad can run from the top of the jacket to armpit level, but if you shoot Skeet or Sporting should run from the top of the shoulder to waist level. This will facilitate gun-mounting, particularly at ISU Skeet. I myself don't like suede shoulder patches on my shooting vests, I feel that smooth, or slightly ribbed, leather gives the best surface for gun-mounting, combined with stability when the gun is mounted.

Make sure that the vest fits reasonably tightly over the clothing you would normally wear whilst shooting. Slack fitting jackets hinder gun-mounting. Light-weight nylon waterproofs will fit under a tight fitting jacket without any problem. At one time if you wanted a smart shooting jacket you had to buy an Italian or American product. This has changed in the last ten years and there are now plenty of smart British made Skeet vests and shooting jackets readily available at most good gun shops. There is no excuse for appearing at a shoot looking like Worzel Gummidge. It is possible to be smartly and functionally dressed, and this all helps to create a better image for our sport, an important point in these times of increased pressure on the shooting sports.

Waterproofs

The United Kingdom is famous the world over for its variable climate, and its quite possible to encounter lashing rain in the middle of summer. To stand on the line soaking wet and shivering does nothing for your chances of winning, so equip yourself with a good set of light-weight waterproofs. Those designed for golfers are ideal for clayshooting. You may find that your normal shooting jacket is a tight fit over waterproofs: if that is the case get one that is slightly larger to fit over your rainsuit.

The waterproof suit will keep your body dry, but don't ignore your feet. There is nothing more miserable than standing on the line in a soaking wet pair of soggy trainers. Get yourself a pair of comfortable waterproof shoes or boots. This does not mean black, farmyard wellies. It is important to ensure that any weatherproof clothing does not restrict your movements or adversely affect your balance or stability. There are a number of fitted boots available on the market and these, or a pair of good, heavy leather shoes should prove suitable in keeping your toes dry.

Cold Weather Clothing

In the last two decades, clayshooting has become an all year round sport. Many of the major shooting grounds hold a Winter Series in a variety of disciplines. Competing in these can mean shooting in snow or sub-zero temperatures. In the past this has usually meant piling on extra sweaters till the shooter resembles a Michelin advert. It does not take much imagination to realize that all these extra layers of clothing must restrict body movement. It's not much good being warm if lack of mobility reduces your scores. Fortunately, the modern clay-shooter has better options than a multiplicity of woollens.

The first thing to get is a set of thermal underwear—vest and long-johns. These are unbelievably effective in keeping the cold out and the warmth in. On top of these wear normal clothing with a thin woollen sweater as a middle layer.

For the top layer, there are a number of quilted shooting jackets available. The best of these come from Canada and are designed to keep out cold infinitely worse than anything you are likely to encounter in Britain. Find a jacket that is comfortable and that doesn't inhibit your gun-handling. To keep the warmth in your legs wear waterproof trousers, and complete the insulation by wearing thermal stockings on your feet, and most importantly, wear a warm hat. This latter is very important, as there is a tremendous heat loss from the head during cold weather.

Following this 'recipe' should ensure that you remain warm during winter competition without suffering any restrictions on your gun-handling.

This immediately gives you an edge over the guy wearing umpteen layers of immobilizing clothing or the poor fellow who is freezing to death in his normal shooting gear. That 'edge' can prove decisive.

Footwear

The feet are very important to successful shooting. They provide the platform on which the body operates. The whole stability of the body depends on your feet having good contact with the ground. To achieve this, suitable footwear is a must.

The majority of shooters seem to favour some form of training or sports shoe. The best of these are ideal, but some of them leave a lot to be desired.

In order that good contact is maintained with the ground, the shoe should have a relatively flat sole. The turned up toes of some training shoes are a liability as they can often cause the feet to rock forward during the swing on to a target. Avoid these turned up toe shoes like the plague. I have found the best form of sports shoe that is readily available are those designed for tennis. The flat sole gives a stable platform from which to shoot, and they're comfortable to wear over a prolonged competition.

There are a number of specialist shooting shoes on the market but these are not readily available in this country. Most of these are designed with a slightly raised heel which keeps the weight well forward on the feet. This is ideal for Trapshooting but I am not sure its such a good idea for Skeet or Sporting. The majority of these shooting shoes are Italian in origin, and have almost certainly been designed with Olympic Trapshooting in mind.

Hearing Protection

The ear is a delicate organ and shooting without adequate hearing protection definitely makes you deaf! This is not speculation, it is fact. Try talking to one of the older generation of shooters who competed in the days when hearing protection was the exception rather than the norm, you'll find that raised voices and a great deal of repetition are required. It cannot be too strongly emphasized that good hearing protection is vital.

There is a wide choice of ear plugs and ear muffs available on the market including highly sophisticated electronic muffs that filter out the harmful noise whilst allowing normal conversation through. Ear muffs provide the most complete protection but some people find them claustrophobic. If this is the case a good pair of ear plugs provides a fair measure of suppression of the dangerous decibels. The best of the ear plugs are those that are custom moulded to each particular ear. These can usually be obtained from any good hearing aid specialist. They are relatively expensive but do provide good protection.

Whilst on the subject of plugs, avoid those that are fitted with a valve that is supposed to filter out the harmful sounds and allow through the lower levels of noise. These are fine in theory, but in practice the valve gets dirty and fails to operate efficiently, drastically reducing the level of protection.

My own preference, when shooting trap, is a pair of comfortable ear muffs and Bilsom cotton wool inserted in the ear. This double measure has an added advantage in that it prevents me hearing extraneous noise from behind the layout. This is a wonderful aid to maintaining complete concentration.

Shooting Glasses

There are two excellent reasons for wearing shooting glasses: to enhance the visibility of the target; and to protect the eyes. The possibility of being struck by a piece of broken target is an ever-present danger when shooting Skeet or Sporting. If that piece of broken target should hit you in the eye, blindness, or seriously impaired vision, is the inevitable result. If you want convincing about the potential danger of target fragments, examine the Low House on a Skeet range. You will find some pretty nasty gashes in the structure caused by target pieces.

Top UIT Skeet shooter, Paul Bentley, tells of the time a piece of target struck his shooting glasses on the right lens during a round of Skeet. The result: damaged glasses, but undamaged right eye. If Paul hadn't been wearing glasses it could have curtailed a brilliant shooting career.

You will note that I have entitled this section 'shooting glasses'. There are a number of specialist shooting glasses available and these are rather different to your Polaroid sunglasses from the local chemist. Shooting glasses are purpose designed for the job in hand and feature frames which are unobtrusive in use and positioned so that the eye looks through the centre of the lens when the gun is mounted to the shoulder. In addition they will have adjustable spring arms that grip securely around the ear, preventing the frame from sliding down the nose under the recoil from the first barrel.

Lens Colours

The idea behind using a variety of different lens tints is to enhance the visibility of targets against various backgrounds. The best colours for specific circumstances will vary from shooter to shooter, and a degree of experimentation is required to determine the optimum for each individual. The following is intended as a rough guide on which to base that experimentation.

Vermilion:
Good for orange targets in medium to bright light conditions.

Blood Red:
Similiar to vermilion, but has the effect of turning orange targets bright yellow. I personally find this an advantage as it seems to remove the 'tail' effect from fluorescent orange targets.

Yellow:
Good for providing target/background contrast on yellow targets.

Gold:
Available in a variety of densities, in its lighter shades, gold is probably the most effective tint for bad light conditions.

Grey:
A good tint for the Skeet shooter where much of the time is spent looking for the target against the glare of the sky. A very light grey tint is also quite effective in dull, cloudy conditions.

Target Orange:
A good all-rounder available in different densities to suit variations in light intensity.

Green:
Similiar properties to grey.

Bronze (Brown):
Excellent in very bright, intense, light conditions.

The foregoing is intended as a guide to help you find the most appropriate lenses for your specific circumstances.

Lenses should preferably be plastic, or of some suitable resin such as CR-39. Such lenses are very resistant to breakage. If glass lenses must be used, then they should be hardened to increase their resistance to impact.

When buying shooting glasses, purchase the very best you can afford. You only have one pair of eyes so ensure that you look after them.

Shooting glasses, especially those with vermilion or red lenses should never be worn as sunglasses as they do not always filter out the harmful effects of strong sunlight. They are an important, and expensive, part of your shooting equipment and should not be exposed to the risks of general wear. People are generally very careless in the way they treat spectacles and it would be disastrous if you sat on your favourite pair of shooting glasses just before your last round. Having, on one occasion, managed to do exactly that, I speak from bitter experience.

It is worth acquiring a pair of good quality sunglasses to wear around the shooting ground in bright conditions. This will reduce exposure to glare which has a fatiguing effect on the body and eyes. Tired eyes will be slower to respond to targets and can also lead to headaches.

Oddments

There are a few additional odds and ends that can help make life more pleasant in our uncertain climate. A pair of good quality leather gloves designed for either shooting or golf will help keep the trigger finger responsive when the temperature plummets. The Sporting shooter will find that a golf umbrella can be a great comfort when queuing to shoot English Sporting stands in the rain, and if you acquire a combined shooting stick/umbrella it enables you to rest your weary feet when queuing in fairer weather. A couple of towels never go amiss: one to keep the gun relatively dry when shooting in a downpour (attach it to the shooting jacket with a safety pin and drape it over the stock and action whilst waiting to shoot), the other to dry yourself on coming in out of the rain. Personally I always keep a change of socks, shirt etc. in one of my shooting bags. No matter how good your waterproofs, persistent rain has a habit of getting in somewhere and wet clothing is a miserable experience at the best of times. A towelling neckerchief can help prevent water finding its way past your collar.

The Shooting Bag

All the aforementioned equipment should be kept in a spacious shooting bag or carryall. Keep it there at all times. If you remove anything—for example to dry it—make sure you return it. Thus, if you pack your shooting bag into the car, you know you are fully equipped.

I always carry two such bags. One with shooting jackets, glasses, earmuffs. The other contains wet and cold weather gear plus a change of clothes. This might appear to be a little over the top, but in 1985 I shot in a selection shoot at Kippen Gun Club in the wettest conditions I have ever competed in. I swore that I would never be that cold, wet and miserable ever again. One cannot select the conditions in which a competition is to be held, so I go equipped to be comfortable whatever the weather. Not only does comfort enhance the performance, but it is well to remember that we shoot for pleasure, not as a penance!

PRE-MATCH PREPARATION

This is vital. It means arriving at a competition in plenty of time with all the equipment you might require. Worrying about the weather because you have left your waterproofs at home is a distraction you can well do without. Likewise, if the competition is over more than one day, make sure your overnight accommodation is booked in advance. You can't concentrate on the job in hand if you are wondering whether you will be sleeping in the car that night. These may seem like minor points, but complete preparation is the foundation on which total confidence is built. If you know that you are prepared for whatever fate may throw at you, then you can channel your entire efforts into winning the match!

The basis, therefore, is to be well prepared. From this point you have to develop a confidence in your ability to win competitions.

PRE-MATCH PRACTICE

Having prepared all your equipment, and having ensured your creature comforts are taken care of, how do you best prepare for the coming competition? It is important to approach a competition feeling confident in your ability to cope with the demands it will make on your shooting skill. One way to ensure this is to practise before the event. Shooters differ in how their performances respond to pre-match practice. Some people benefit from a lot, others require very little. My own preference is to shoot quite a bit before an important event. I don't practise much other than before a shoot. I find the best form of practice is to shoot competition. There is little point in just blazing away for the sake of it. Plan your practice around a specific event and try to ensure that the latter part is shot on the actual competition ground. If possible shoot at least one round on each layout.

It is not always possible to practise at this sort of level. Some shooting grounds offer very limited opportunities for practise, and it is very rare to be allowed to practise on the ground before a Sporting competition. Nevertheless, if you can't get to practise on the ground, make sure you get some shooting in during the week before the competition. Just a few shots will keep the gun feeling part of you, and the familiarity that comes from regular handling of your gun(s) is extremely beneficial. If you haven't picked up a gun since your last competition it's likely to feel rather strange for the first few shots until you settle down. You could easily miss a target or two while you're doing that 'settling in'.

THE PSYCHOLOGY
OF SHOOTING

Perhaps the 'Psychology of Shooting' is too grand a title for this chapter. I am not a qualified psychologist, but it did not take me long to realize that the mental approach to shooting was every bit as important as the physical ability to hit targets consistently. There are a good many talented shooters in this country who can return brilliant scores in practice and minor competitions, but who fall by the wayside when it comes to selection shoots and major championships. This is not due to inadequacies in their shooting technique, but is the result of a lack of ability in dealing with match pressure. I have always felt that the difference between the top four or five shooters and the rest is nothing to do with skill with a gun. The consistent winners appear to have a much stronger desire to succeed and it is that will to win that gives them the edge over the rest of the field.

So how do you rise to their level? The first thing you must realize about individual sports such as shooting is that the real competition is between you and the target. If you hit every target that appears you can't be beaten! So you must strive to hit every single target. Your whole concentration must be focused on that one thing. To achieve this you must have confidence in your own ability. When you call for a bird you must know in your own mind that if you do everything correctly you WILL break the target. The basis of a good mental approach to the sport is a high level of technical skill. It should be instinctive to shoot correctly. You must not be thinking about the technicalities of shooting when you should be concentrating on seeing and hitting the target. To achieve this you must hone your level of skill to a point where all you have to think about when competing is the winning.

To get to this point requires some considerable effort and preparation (see Competition Preparation, p.127).

THE PRESSURE OF COMPETITION

Pressure is experienced by everyone in a competitive situation: it is how you handle it that determines how successful you will be. So many top shooters make it look so effortless when shooting well, that a lot of people believe that the top boys have no nerves at all. This, of course, is entirely wrong: the men at the top have just learned how to cope with and control the nervous tension so that any adverse effect on their performance is minimized.

To deal with pressure, it's important to identify what causes it. In the overwhelming majority of cases it is a fear of missing, and consequent to this, a fear of losing, and worse still a fear of being seen to lose. Failure is bad enough, but failing in front of your fellow competitors is even worse. To excuse this we come up with some wonderful remarks such as 'I only shoot for fun', 'I wasn't trying', or 'the result isn't important'. If it's not important, how come people get so nervous? No, the truth is that most of us, underneath, are subconsciously afraid of failure.

To overcome this you have to realize that it is possible to control pressure and make it work for you. When you are under pressure in a competitive situation your body reacts with the 'flight or fight' response of the caveman confronted with danger. Competition is really a civilized substitute for danger. The 'fight or flight' syndrome causes changes in your body's chemistry—sugar and adrenalin are released into the blood and the body assumes a state of readiness to engage battle. This is a normal reaction to pressure and it can actually improve your performance. Your primary senses of touch and vision become more acute, and your abilities to judge speed and distance are intensified.

If you don't believe this, think about those occasions when you are shooting really well. The targets appear slow and you seem to have all the time in the world to deal with them. It almost seems as if time has slowed down for you. This happens when you have the body's responses under control and are making them work for you. Contrast this with those situations when things go wrong. Then the targets seem to be going a million miles an hour and the harder you try the worse things get. This is when the level of anxiety rises to such a degree that it disturbs your confidence and as the level of fear rises, panic sets in and things go off the rails. At this stage it's very easy to start believing that you can't hit the targets consistently, and if that occurs, you'll very quickly prove yourself right!

So, how can we channel this pressure to work for you? The secret is in preparation followed by some very positive thinking.

Firstly, prepare yourself for the fray from the moment you get up in the morning. Give yourself plenty of time to do all the things you want to before you leave for the shoot. It is not good preparation to be rushing out to the car, unshaven, cramming toast into your mouth, and wondering if you'll make the start time. Racing around frantically at the start of the day induces an unnecessary state of anxiety from which it is hard to recover. You should have plenty of time to shower, shave, eat breakfast, load the car with all your gear and leave in plenty of time to reach the ground without driving like Ayrton Senna. This will place you on the shooting ground, fully equipped and fully prepared and in a relatively relaxed frame of mind.

Secondly, get yourself to the layout in plenty of time before each round. Check you have got everything and have a look at the targets. Don't sit in the clubhouse till the last possible minute and then have to run for the line. At best this leaves you ill-prepared and harassed, at worst it can mean you miss your squad and incur a three target penalty.

Once on the stand, compose yourself and start building up your determination to succeed. You must tackle each target individually. Treat the competition as a one bird match – the next one. Provided you keep hitting the next target you will be invincible.

Learn to channel your concentration. At Sporting it's pretty obvious that you give it maximum concentration from the moment you step on to the stand until you walk off again. As you come off the stand switch off the concentration. Skeet is very similiar in this respect. Give it your all when you are actually on the station, but let your mind freewheel whilst not shooting. Trap, however, is slightly different. Because of the shooting format of the Trap disciplines, the shooter feels locked into the round

from the word go. There is no opportunity to wander off and relax a little once the shooting has started. This often results in a shooter trying to maintain maximum concentration throughout the entire round. Now, the duration of the maximum concentration span of the average human is about 15 minutes. A round of Olympic Trap takes about 25 minutes. It's quite easy to deduce from this that your concentration will run out of steam before the end of the round if you keep it turned up to maximum all the time. The answer is to put your concentration into 'stand-by' mode between shots. After you eject your cartridges relax a little, let your mind float, and only start turning on the concentration again as the shooter two places to your left closes his gun. This ebbing and flowing of effort should enable you to focus your concentration where it is most needed, into your shooting effort.

In learning how to concentrate, learn how to eliminate outside distractions as far as possible. If something does disturb you as you are about to shoot, take the gun down and start your preparation all over again. Don't attempt to call a target while your mind is somewhere else. In the same manner, don't let yourself be distracted by missing. If a target slips away remain calm. There is nothing to be gained by losing your temper and a great deal to be lost—including other targets! Letting anger take over when your performance slips is a sure way of damaging your chances in the remainder of the round. Focus your attention on the next target, remember, whether you have hit or missed, the previous targets are history and there is nothing you can do to change them. A loss of temper is a loss of control and you need to remain totally in control to succeed.

There are times when all this will come naturally, without conscious effort on your part. At such times shooting seems easy. The mark of a true winner is the ability to succeed when the mental part of the game doesn't come easily. It's fine to produce a dazzling performance when everything is going your way, but the human condition being what it is, this wonderful state won't occur every time you go to shoot. I remember listening to an interview with Steve Davies during the World Snooker Championship in which he summed this up perfectly. Steve said that to be Number One required not only winning when everything is right, but the ability to drag a winning performance out of yourself when everything seems to be going against you. To do this requires an awful lot of positive thinking. The human subconscious is a wonderful ally but can become a formidable enemy when the doubts start to creep in. If you start to believe in your ability to succeed then your conscious mind will come to dominate the subconscious.

So be positive, believe in yourself. Tell yourself you can win despite the fact that you don't feel at your brightest, and keep telling yourself till you believe it. If you let the doubts take hold then you are doomed. Doubts have a habit of feeding on themselves. Left unchecked they multiply and things get worse in a self-perpetuating cycle.

WINNING

The time will come when you are in a position to win for the first time. Perhaps you are leading the shoot with one round to go. At this point the easiest thing you can do is lose! This usually happens because you lose confidence in your capability to go on and win. You become frightened of failure. The fear and the doubt combine to cause the very thing you are afraid of. This is where positive thought comes in. You must tell yourself that you certainly can win. You have proved it by the fact that you are in the lead. You shooting is good enough to be leading so it is good enough to go on to win.

I have heard shooters say that they don't like the pressure of leading the shoot, especially overnight in a two or three day match. They prefer to come from behind at the finish. This is absolute nonsense. The real pressure is on the man behind. If you are in the lead, you at least have a margin for error, and the fact that you are out in front means that you are shooting better than your rivals. To come from behind means that they must rely on the leader making mistakes. He may, but then he may not. Relying on other peoples mistakes is a very uncertain path to success.

The best position to be is out in front. Once you are there you are controlling the situation. Just keep plodding along and the rest of the field (or your class) have to struggle to keep up. You may think you are under pressure, but believe me the shooters behind you are under far more pressure. Thay can't afford to make any errors because that will increase your lead. Take comfort in this situation and your cofidence will grow. As your fellow competitors see that leading the shoot doesn't bother you, their confidence will start to slip. You will be making them believe that they can't win. It is all a question of inducing the right frame of mind, and practice in this form of positive thinking will enable you to win when the chance presents itself.

When you are in this leading position you will often find that your nearest rivals will appear, as if by magic, behind the line when you are going on to shoot. Don't let this put you off. Don't pretend not to see them. It doesn't matter if they know that you are aware of their presence. The fatal mistake in this situation is to start mentally ticking off targets. You know the sort of thing 'if I miss one so and so will be tied with me'. If you start thinking this you are not concentrating on your shooting and you are letting your opponents distract you. When this happens a miss is not long in coming.

Concentrate on making a good job of the shooting. Let the presence of your rivals spur you on. Instead of being distracted be determined to annihilate every target. You'll soon forget the people standing behind and at the end of the round you will have turned the tables on them. Instead of pressurizing you, they will have demoralized themselves. Just appearing cool and in command of the situation starts the doubts creeping into your rivals' minds.

The Scoreboard

This is there to record the scores for everyone to see. An obvious statement but it never ceases to surprise me how many shooters take on the scoreboard as an extra adversary. You see them pacing around watching everybody's scores as they come in. By the time it's their turn to shoot they have worked themselves into a rare old state. Instead of getting on with their own shooting, they're thinking about everyone else's. As a result their concentration slips, and targets start escaping. So don't let the scoreboard be your enemy. Ignore it till the end and look at it to see where you stand.

Shooting in Teams

Hopefully the time will come in your shooting career when you qualify for a team. This may be a club team or a national one. Whichever, you will justifiably feel proud of yourself. This pride will be tempered by a desire not to let the team down. Team

THE PSYCHOLOGY OF SHOOTING

competition in the shooting sports is a strange thing. Shooting is not a team sport: when you are standing out there on the shooting station, the only person who can help you is yourself. The actions of your team-mates have no relevance to your performance on the line.

Personally, I have found the best approach to team competition is to ignore it. Concentrate on your individual performance, and if this is successful you will have done your share by the team. This may sound a little selfish but it does take a lot of pressure off you. When you are on the line you need to be devoting maximum concentration to your shooting. Worrying about letting down your team-mates, or making up the deficit if one of them has slipped a little, is not conducive to good shooting and simply puts you under extra pressure you can well do without. Team spirit is an important ingredient to team success, but encouraging each other should not involve a shot by shot analysis of the team's position during the competition. There is plenty of time for post-mortems when the match is concluded. Encourage your colleagues to perform well as individuals and let the team score take care of itself.

The previous remarks about the scoreboard apply even more to team competitions. Time and again the British team has lost team medals on the last round because members become too concerned about the result and put increased pressure on themselves. If each member of the team concentrates on his own individual shooting and ignores the opposition then the chances of success are greatly increased.

Shoot-Offs

At some time or other in your competitive shooting it is likely that you will be confronted with a shoot-off. Indeed the new Olympic style Final is almost a shoot-off. The important thing is to remain calm and in control. Easier said than done. You will naturally be anxious but you must not let this anxiety affect your shooting. There are ways of reducing the pressure on yourself.

Firstly, don't let any doubts creep in about your shooting ability. You must be shooting equally as well as your opponent. The fact that you are tied with him proves this. So reassure yourself that you can handle him purely on a shooting level.

Secondly, don't let other people hype you up. Take yourself off somewhere quiet and relax until it's time to shoot. Getting all worked up before the shoot off is counterproductive. You don't need sky-high adrenalin levels to win a shoot-off. What you do need is to be quietly determined and totally in control. Whatever you do, don't boast about how you are going to win beforehand. That really is tempting fate. It's much better to let your gun do the talking for you. No one looks sillier than a braggart who fails. It's one thing to savour success but you need to be very sure of yourself before you start predicting it.

My own way of controlling pressure when confronted with a shoot-off is to look at what has been achieved so far. If I am tied for first place with, say, two other shooters, I think to myself: 'The worst that can happen is that I'll come third in the shoot. That's a pretty good result—now here's a chance to improve on it.' I find this approach helps keep the pressure off prior to the shoot off. Obviously I want to win but the realisation of what I have achieved thus far has a calming effect on me.

Once the shoot-off commences it is simply a matter of shooting in the same manner as you did during the competition.

One of the danger times during a shoot-off is the moment when your opponent misses. It is very easy for relief to cause you to relax slightly with the result that you miss the next target yourself. When an opponent misses, I always pause momentarily and almost 'stoke up' my determination to destroy the next target. This usually results in the next target being totally obliterated, something that I hope is as disheartening to the opposition as it encouraging to me.

One final point on shoot-offs. If a coin is spun to decide the order of shooting, and you are fortunate to win the toss, always elect to shoot first. It's much better to lead from the front and let your opponent chase your score. Many a shoot off has been won or lost on the last target,

so given the choice, let the other guy be the last to shoot.

REDUCING TENSION

The constant theme in this chapter has been to keep anxiety and tension under control. How can you best do this? Well, there are a few little tricks that can help you. Firstly, as has been said previously, prepare completely from the outset. If you are sure that you are completely equipped for the competition then that is one less thing to worry about. Worry increases tension and you'll get enough of that from the actual shooting without wondering whether you have packed your favourite shooting glasses or not.

Secondly, during the match take time off to relax. Sit in the car and listen to the radio, read a newspaper or a book, or even have a short snooze. Don't spend the time between rounds wandering about the shooting stations looking at everbody else in action. The sound of gunfire can induce fatigue so remove yourself from it. You really shouldn't spend any more time close to the shooting ranges than is absolutely necessary. Whatever you do, avoid getting into heated discussions about shooting. This sort of thing just drains the mind and your concentration will suffer. If you start to feel tense just before shooting, sit down quietly and take a few deep breaths. Force yourself to relax. Tension can help you produce good scores, in fact a little bit of tension is absolutely vital to success, but if it gets out of hand it can have a very detrimental effect on your performance. So learn to control it.

When competing in events that take part over more than one day, make sure you relax in the evening. Sitting in the hotel bar talking shooting is most definitely not relaxing. Haven't you had enough of shooting on the range? Switch yourself off totally from anything to do with shooting: watch the television or go to the cinema, play tennis, go fishing—anything but 'shooting'. This will ensure that you wake up refreshed and ready for the fray. By the way, relaxing doesn't mean trying to empty the beer cellar in the hotel. Personally, I rarely drink in the evening when competing. Probably the odd drink won't hurt but any substantial intake of alcohol can't be good for your shooting – or your liver!

Kevin Gill, winner of a gold medal with Ian Peel in the Olympic Trap Pairs event and a silver medal in the Olympic Trap Individual event at the New Zealand Commonwealth Games in 1990.

As I said at the beginning, psychology is too grand a title for this chapter, but I hope that some of the advice helps you sort out a more positive mental approach to the game. It's far more important than the majority of clayshooters realize. Ask the people who appear in the medals year after year.

THE LAW

The Firearms (Amendment) Act 1988 introduced significant changes in the certification procedure for shotguns in the United Kingdom. These are the requirements.

THE SHOTGUN CERTIFICATE

In order to possess or acquire a shotgun it is necessary to apply to the police for a Shotgun Certificate. Under the 1968 **Firearms Act**, a Chief Constable HAD to issue a certificate unless he could show that the applicant:

    i. Had a criminal record
    ii. Was a danger to the public safety or
    iii. Was insane.

There was no requirement to show a need for a gun, or proof of club membership or permission to shoot. This has changed somewhat under the 1988 Act. An applicant is now required to have a reason for possessing a shotgun. The 1988 Act states:

'an applicant shall, in particular, be regarded as having a good reason if the gun is intended to be used for sporting or competition purposes or for shooting vermin; and an application shall not be refused merely because the applicant intends neither to use the gun himself nor lend it for anyone else to use.'

Any regular clayshooter should have no problems with this part of the new Act. You do not have to provide the police with written permission to shoot or evidence of club membership on your application.

Section 7.6 of '**Firearms Law: Guidance to the Police**' (issued by **the Home Office**) declares :

'A Chief Officer should therefore need to make further enquiries only where it comes to his notice that there may be genuine doubts about an applicant's reasons for possessing a shotgun.'

This clearly implies that police enquiries will only be extended if they have real doubts about your intentions. Anybody reading this book with the intention of improving their competition shooting should have little trouble in obtaining or renewing a Shotgun Certificate.

Application for a Certificate

The application is made on a form obtainable from your local Police station.

The new forms require four passport-sized photographs to be submitted with the application. One of these photographs has to be authenticated by a referee, who must also declare that he has known you for at least two years and that he knows of no reason why you should not own a shotgun.

This referee must be a UK resident. As with a passport application, he or she has to be an MP, magistrate, minister of religion, lawyer, doctor, bank manager, established civil servant or person of a similiar standing. Quite who qualifies as a 'person of similiar standing' has yet to be decided but any member of the Professions or an officer in one of the services should prove suitable. Please note that this reference is not just applicable to the initial application, in future you will have to get a referee and photographs every time you renew your certificate.

You will also have to furnish details of all shotguns possessed at the time of the application. These will be listed, by the police in Table 1 of the new shotgun certificate. There is no limit on the number of guns you may hold under the new legislation, but any new guns acquired during the life of the certificate must be entered in Table 2. Any acquisitions must be notified to your local police force within seven days, giving details of the gun (make, serial number etc.), and the name and address of the previous owner. Likewise, if you dispose of any of your guns, unless it is to a Registered Firearms Dealer, you must notify the police within seven days that the gun has been disposed of. You must also enter details of the gun on the certificate of the recipient. There is provision in the new law for the loan of guns. If you wish to borrow a gun for a period of less than 72 hours, there is no requirement to notify the police provided the lender and the borrower hold shotgun certificates.

Before the 1988 Act came into force, anyone over the age of 17 could legally purchase shotgun ammunition regardless of whether they held a Shotgun Certificate or not. This has now changed. You are now required to produce your certificate when acquiring ammunition. There is no limit on the amounts you may hold and the details are not entered on the certificate as they would be in the case of rifle or pistol ammunition. If you wish someone else to purchase ammunition on your behalf, this is permitted provided you authorize them in writing and they take your Shotgun Certificate with them. Certain types of shotgun ammunition require a Firearms Certificate for their possession and acquisition, but these cartridges are not used for clayshooting. Any cartridge which complies with the rules of the UIT, FITASC, CPSA **et al** is freely available to Shotgun Certificate holders.

143

PUMP-ACTION AND SEMI-AUTOMATIC SHOTGUNS

The 1988 Act redefined the status of repeating shotguns. Previously there was no restriction on these weapons other than the normal one of barrel length (all smooth-bore guns must have a barrel length of 24in to be classed as a shotgun within the meaning of the 1968 Act). As of 1 January 1990, repeating shotguns must have their magazines limited to a maximum of two cartridges. This must be done in an approved manner and submitted to one of the Proof Houses for certification and marking. If this is done the gun may be retained on a Shotgun Certificate. If you wish to keep a repeating shotgun with a greater magazine capacity, then you will have to apply to the police for a Firearms Certificate. One important point here, the shotgun classification only applies to guns with a fixed magazine. If your gun has a detachable magazine, regardless of capacity, then it is classed as a Part 1. firearm which requires a Firearm Certificate.

SECURITY

The old style Shotgun Certificate carried only two conditions: that the holder sign it in ink; and that he notify the Chief Constable of the theft or loss of any shotguns. There was no mention of security such as is found on a Firearms Certificate. Although security was not mandatory, all responsible gun owners took care to ensure that their guns were kept safe and out of unauthorised hands. The 1988 **Firearms (Amendment) Act** changed this, so that certificates bear the following conditions:

A. The shotguns to which the certificate relates must at all times (except in the circumstances set out in paragraph B below) be stored securely so as to prevent, so far as is reasonably practicable, access to the guns by an unauthorised person.

B. Where a shotgun to which the certificate relates is in use or the holder of the certificate has the shotgun with him for the purpose of cleaning, repairing or testing it or for some other purpose connected with its use, transfer or sale, or the gun is in transit to or from a place in connection with its use or any such purpose, reasonable precautions must be taken for the safe custody of the gun.

So now there is a statutory requirement to keep your gun safe and out of unauthorised hands.

The best way to summarize this requirement is to quote from the Home Office 'Guidance to the Police':

Condition A. Secure storage

'Storage should be in a locked gun cabinet or other similiar secure container. However, in deciding on the appropriate level of security, chief officers will wish to have regard to the individual circumstances in each case. In some cases, removal and secure storage of firing mechanisms will be an acceptable alternative to use of a gun cabinet.

Where a cabinet is used, it should be in a protected part of the premises (not in a garage or outhouse), out of sight of casual visitors, and securely fixed to the fabric of the building. A gun room offering a comparable level of security, or a cellar with a lockable steel door, would be satisfactory alternatives.'

Condition B. Security in use or transit

'Compliance with the requirements under paragraph B of the Security Condition must be viewed in the light of the circumstances. It should not normally be neccessary to insist upon a security device in cars when guns and ammunition are only transported infrequently. If the vehicle is to be left unattended it will normally be sufficient for the bolt, trigger mechanism or foreend of the gun to be removed where practicable and for the remainder of the gun and ammunition to be concealed from view in the locked vehicle.

If the vehicle is to be left unattended for prolonged periods, it may be better (in appropriate circum- stances) to remove the guns and keep them on the person or in some other more secure place if available.'

From this, it can be seen that gun security is being taken a lot more seriously. However, there should be no real problem for the clayshooter. In all probability the local police will require you to store your guns in a steel gun cabinet, but this is a sensible precaution anyway. After all good competition guns do not come cheap!

The 1988 legislation, although it may be inconvenient at times, should pose no difficulties to the law abiding citizen. If you are in any doubt, or have any difficulty on this matter, the British Shooting Sports Council or the firearms officer at the headquarters of the British Association for Shooting and Conservation should be able to help and advise you.

INSURANCE

There is no legal requirement for Public Liability insurance covering the use of shotguns, but you would be well advised to take out cover. Membership of the CPSA, SCPA, UCPSA, WCTSA and BASC all include Public Liability insurance that covers your sporting shooting. This is one good reason to join one of the above associations. If you are not a member (and you should be), contact the CPSA's insurance advisor, Mr Norman Cooper to arrange suitable cover.

Heaven forbid that you should ever have an accident with a shotgun, but if the unthinkable happened, good insurance cover would be vital. A personal injury claim could involve large sums of money and lack of proper insurance could leave you personally liable.

In the same vein, always ensure that any shooting ground you visit has suitable insurance cover. If it doesn't, shoot somewhere else! The vast majority of decent shooting grounds will have more than adequate cover but some of the smaller clubs and grounds may be deficient.

CONCLUSION

In the twenty-one years I have been competing seriously at clayshooting there have been many changes in the sport. When I first started shooting clays, Down-The Line was the dominant discipline, and Sporting and English Skeet were very popular in certain parts of the country, but the International disciplines were very poorly attended. Gradually this has changed and Sporting is now, without doubt, the most popular form of clay target shooting; while FITASC Sporting has become an established part of the shooting scene. There has been an upsurge of interest in the other International disciplines. The first British Grand Prix Olympic Trap that I took part in (1971) attracted around 40 entries. The 1989 British Grand Prix had an entry of 216 with many more on a waiting list. The majority of the major championships in 1989 were over subscribed, many having a full entry weeks before the competition. This sounds as if the sport is in a very healthy state, and I suppose in many ways it is. Yet shooting is coming under increasing pressure from a number of quarters.

Changing firearms legislation in Britain, together with occasional media hype, could have a dramatic effect on the numbers of people who shoot and their freedom to do so. Once again, I cannot overemphasize the importance of safety considerations at every occasion. Individual shooters, as well as their national organizations, have a responsibility to ensure the continuance of their sport through their own responsible actions. The best way of refuting hostile press attention is through action and continued emphasis on safety, as well as through reasoned debate in media channels.

On the plus side, clayshooting has received some beneficial media attention in Britain in the form of **Starshot**. The televising of David Maxwell's 'made for telly' clayshooting attracted large audiences and put an 'acceptable' face of shooting across to the public. I heard a lot of favourable comments about **Starshot** from non-shooters. This has to be good for clayshooting. Apart from encouraging some people to take up the sport, it showed viewers what a challenging and demanding sport clayshooting is. This helps people to understand the attraction of shooting as a sport and this form of passive support must be beneficial to us.

Another growth area in clayshooting is the corporate shooting day. Many companies have taken to clayshooting as a means of entertaining their clients, who come along for some basic tuition, a small competition and some fairly lavish wining and dining, usually in a beautiful country house setting. Clayshooting is an ideal medium for company entertaining. Guests require no experience of the sport and the coaches employed by the major operators in this field will soon have absolute beginners hitting clays. Clayshooting is one of the few sports at which the complete novice can be immediately successful and thoroughly enjoy himself. Again this has an important spin off for the whole sport. Many of the people who attend these days will never have shot before. Some of them will go on to take up the sport, but those who don't will have enjoyed themselves and will have an understanding of the attractions of shooting. Thus a few more passive supporters of our sport are created. The more that members of the public understand the attractions of clayshooting, the more secure our future.

Unfortunately we are also under attack from another quarter. The environmentalist lobby has taken against shooting on the grounds of noise and 'pollution'. Many councils are very reluctant to grant planning permission for new shooting grounds and some of them have made life exceedingly difficult for existing ones. The Department of the Environment, in a surprise move at the end of 1988, brought in a measure to limit the number of days a site could be used for clayshooting without planning permission. Prior to their move clubs were allowed to shoot for up to 28 days a year without planning consent. At a stroke this was reduced to 14 days. There was no prior consultation and it looked as if the smaller clubs and shooting grounds, the backbone of our sport, were going to have their shooting halved. Fortunately for once the shooting organizations got their act together and put immense pressure on the Minister of State so that he eventually capitulated and reverted to 28 days. This just goes to show what can be done with a bit of unified action! However this does not prevent local councils severely restricting or closing shooting grounds on the basis of noise pollution. Sometimes they are justified because of the thoughtlessness of shoot organisers, but in many cases the complaints are spurious to say the least. This is a problem that is not going to go away and vigilance is required to prevent shooting grounds and clubs being closed unnecessarily.

There is also pressure on us to replace the lead in shotgun cartridges with some other less toxic metal. There has been a lot of misinformation about the problem of lead pollution. The primary danger is one of wildfowl ingesting lead pellets when dibbling in shallow water. Not too many clubs shoot over shallow lakes where waterfowl feed. The idea that lead

Sponsorship is vital to the future development of the sport. Sponsors must be looked after and made welcome by all shooters.

dissolves into the soil and thus gets into the human and animal food chain, is, I am reliably informed, scientifically unsound. Apparently lead is a chemically inert substance in the solid form and does not readily dissolve in normal circumstances. Perhaps it may if subjected to huge quantities of acidic rainfall, but then surely the problem is the acid rain, not the lead pellets! If lead dissolved readily all those church roofs that have been up for hundreds of years would have dissolved away years ago. The shooting community needs to be more positive in its approach to this one. There needs to be some proper scientific research into the subject. Couldn't the cartridge manu-facturers get together on this and fund a research project? Surely it would be to their ultimate benefit. Otherwise we might face the prospect of having our chokes bulged by the use of steel shot.

The real cloud on the horizon is the fact that many of these issues have been taken on board by the EEC. Swingeing proposals that could seriously limit the development of any new shooting grounds are currently under consideration in Brussels. This only strengthens the argument for some properly conducted, properly funded, serious research into these problems. We have to know the facts if we are going to successfully defend our sport.

Finally a quick look at how our sport is managed. In the UK clay-shooting is administered by the four home associations: the Clay Pigeon Shooting Association (England), the Scottish Clay Pigeon Association, the Ulster Clay Pigeon Shooting Association, and the Welsh Clay Target Shooting Association. Each is responsible for the administration and development of the sport in their respective countries and all are, by and large, run by amateurs. The English CPSA is far and away the largest of the four bodies.

British representation at international level is governed by the British CPSA's International Board, composed of representatives from the four home associations plus members elected by the international shooters at their AGM. While the weekend or average clayshooter will have little contact with these organizations, except in arranging shooting insurance and in communicating over changes in regulations of individual clay disciplines or cartridge weights (all of which can and is usually carried out by your local gun club or shooting school), these organizations do attract criticism from some members of the international clayshooting community – myself included – for not holding the shooters' interests close enough to heart in their decision making processes. It is really only with the shooters and the organizations working together that we can carry the sport of clayshooting forward and take on the challenges facing the sport in the years to come.

The 1988 World FITASC Sporting Champion, John Bidwell from Suffolk, England.

APPENDICES

THE ASSOCIATIONS

The Clay Pigeon Shooting
   Association,
107 Epping New Road,
Buckhurst Hill,
Essex IG9 5TG.
01–505–6221.

The Scottish Clay Pigeon Association,
10 Balgibbon,
Collander,
Perthshire.

The Ulster Clay Pigeon Shooting
   Association,
6, Springhill Avenue,
Bangor,
County Down BT20 3NT
0247–463–153

The Welsh Clay Target Shooting
   Association,
Arbroath,
45 Picton Road,
Hakin,
Milford Haven,
South Wales.

As the Ulster, Scottish and Welsh
Associations have no permanent
offices these addresses are liable to
change. In case of difficulty contact
the CPSA for the current address.

Europe and the US

The International Shooting Union.
   (ISU or UIT)
UIT,
Bavariaring 21,
D–8000 Munchen 2,
Federal Republic of Germany.
(0 89) 53 10 12.

Federation Internationale de Tir aux
   Armes Sportive de Chasse,
   (FITASC)
10 Rue de Lisbonne,
Paris 75008,
France.

Federazione Italiana Tiro A Volo,
   (FITAV)
Viala Tiziano 70,
00100 Roma,
Italy.

Amateur Trapshooting Association,
   (ATA)
601 W. National Rd.,
Vandalia,
Ohio 45377,
United States of America.

United States Sporting Clays
    Association,
50 Briar Hollow,
Suite 490 East,
Houston,
TX 77027,
United States of America.

METRIC/IMPERIAL
EQUIVALENTS

Barrel Length:		Weight:	
66cm	26in	2800g	6lb 3oz
68cm	26¾in	2900g	6lb 6oz
70cm	27⅝in	3000g	6lb 10oz
72cm	28⅜in	3200g	7lb 1oz
74cm	29¼in	3300g	7lb 4oz
75cm	29½in	3500g	7lb 12oz
76cm	30in	3600g	7lb 15oz
80cm	31½in	3700g	8lb 3oz
81cm	32in	3800g	8lb 6oz
86cm	34in	4000g	8lb 13oz

Olympic Trap range
at the Perazzi factory.

Perazzi interchangeable chokes.

BIBLIOGRAPHY

The following books should prove of interest. They are all titles that I have found enjoyable and informative. Some of them are out of print but a diligent search of the secondhand sporting book trade should turn up most of them. There are one or two that might prove difficult to locate, and I am greatly indebted to my old friend Chris Craddock for his help in obtaining some of the rarer titles in my own collection.

Robert ARTHUR **The Shotgun Stock**
Maj. Charles ASKINS **The Shotgunner's Book**
Paul BENTLEY **Clay Target Shooting**
Capt. Adam H. BOGARDUS **Field, Cover and Trapshooting**
John BRINDLE **Shotguns and Shooting**
Bob BRISTER **Shotgunning, The Art and the Science**
Chris CRADDOCK **A Manual of Clayshooting**
Fred ETCHEN **Commonsense Shotgun Shooting**
W.W. GREENER **The Breechloader and How to Use it**
Elmer KEITH **Shotguns**
Charles LANCASTER **The Art of Shooting**
Fred MISSILDENE **Score Better at Trap**
Fred MISSILDENE **Score Better at Skeet**
André MONTAGUE **Successful Shotgun Shooting**
Bob NICHOLLS **The Shotgunner**
Michael RAYMONT **Modern Clay Pigeon Shooting**
Mike REYNOLDS **Shooting Made Easy**
G.W. SPEARING **The Craft of the Gunsmith**
A.J. 'Smoker' SMITH **Sporting Clays**
Jack LEWIS & Jack MITCHELL **2nd Shotgun Digest**
Robert STACK **Shotgun Digest**
Percy STANBURY & Gordon CARLISLE **Shotgun Marksmanship**
L.R. WALLACK **American Shotgun Design and Performance**
Roderick WILLET **The Good Shot**
Gerhard WIRNSBERGER **The Standard Directory of Proof Marks**
Don ZUTZ **The Double Shotgun**

All these books should prove interesting to the clayshooter, but there is one that is a 'must'. That is Bob Brister's 'Shotgunning, the Art and the Science'. This is quite the most interesting book on shotgunning I have come across.

INDEX

156